Jesus is the most disruptive person who ever lived, because he's always focused on growth, not on perpetuating the status quo. Likewise, my Jesus-loving friend Carl Medearis is one of the most disruptive people I've ever met—you'll see what I mean when you read *42 Seconds*. These short bursts of truth, at times hilarious and at times profound, will move you deeper into a lifestyle that produces fruit in others' lives. Listen and learn from Carl, and you'll leave the status quo behind for something like an epic adventure.

RICK LAWRENCE, author of *The Jesus-Centered Life*, general editor of the *Jesus-Centered Bible*, and host of the podcast *Paying Ridiculous Attention to Jesus*

I am a big fan of Carl Medearis. He's always fun yet challenging, provocative yet deeply biblical. In *42 Seconds*, he is no different. Exploring the art of getting to the point with people just like Jesus did is so necessary in our present cultural moment. You will be blessed and challenged by this book.

DANIEL FUSCO, pastor of Crossroads Community Church (Vancouver, WA, and Portland, OR) and author of *Upward, Inward, Outward* and *Honestly*

Carl Medearis does it again. He brings enormous ideas down to earth where we all live and helps us to see how—as Dallas Willard used to say—"We can live our lives the way Jesus would live our lives . . . if Jesus had our lives to live." And Jesus is supposed to have our lives to live. Carl brings amazingly simple, insightful, and practical suggestions directly from the life of Jesus . . . and offers them to us to practice in our real, everyday lives.

BART TARMAN, speaker, artist, and former chaplain of Westmont College

It's amazing how often our words and actions can make the Good News Jesus proclaimed and embodied sound and look like Bad News. Our world is in desperate need of Jesus people to take seriously our invitation to speak, think, and act in ways reflective of the One we follow. In this book, Carl offers a relatable, thoughtful, and extremely tangible guide for how to not only say we believe in the Good News but also narrate it with our lives.

JON HUCKINS, pastor and coauthor of *Mend*

42

SECONDS

THE JESUS MODEL FOR EVERYDAY INTERACTIONS

CARL MEDEARIS

A NavPress resource published in alliance
with Tyndale House Publishers, Inc.

NavPress is the publishing ministry of The Navigators, an international Christian organization and leader in personal spiritual development. NavPress is committed to helping people grow spiritually and enjoy lives of meaning and hope through personal and group resources that are biblically rooted, culturally relevant, and highly practical.

For more information, visit www.NavPress.com.

42 Seconds: The Jesus Model for Everyday Interactions

Copyright © 2018 by Carl Medearis. All rights reserved.

A NavPress resource published in alliance with Tyndale House Publishers, Inc.

NAVPRESS and the NAVPRESS logo are registered trademarks of NavPress, The Navigators, Colorado Springs, CO. *TYNDALE* is a registered trademark of Tyndale House Publishers, Inc. Absence of ® in connection with marks of NavPress or other parties does not indicate an absence of registration of those marks.

The Team:
Don Pape, Publisher
Caitlyn Carlson, Acquisitions Editor
Cara Iverson, Copy Editor
Dan Farrell, Designer

Cover photograph of men copyright © Sparky2000/iStockphoto. All rights reserved.

Some of the anecdotal illustrations in this book are true to life and are included with the permission of the persons involved. All other illustrations are composites of real situations, and any resemblance to people living or dead is purely coincidental.

For information about special discounts for bulk purchases, please contact Tyndale House Publishers at csresponse@tyndale.com, or call 1-800-323-9400.

Cataloging-in-Publication Data is available.

ISBN 978-1-63146-489-8

Printed in the United States of America

24   23   22   21   20   19   18
7   6   5   4   3   2   1

CONTENTS

Introduction *vii*

1 BE KIND

CHAPTER ONE: Say Hey *3*
CHAPTER TWO: Acknowledge the Waiter *7*
CHAPTER THREE: Ask Another Question *13*
CHAPTER FOUR: Do Something Small *21*
CHAPTER FIVE: Talk to the Kid *27*
      The Final Word: "Be Kind" 31

2 BE PRESENT

CHAPTER SIX: Breathe Deep *35*
CHAPTER SEVEN: Stop Trying to Be Cool *43*
CHAPTER EIGHT: Open Your Eyes and Ears *49*
CHAPTER NINE: Accept That You Are Not God *55*
CHAPTER TEN: Don't Be So Strategic *59*
      The Final Word: "Be Present" 67

3 BE BRAVE

CHAPTER ELEVEN: Find Your Barley Field *75*
CHAPTER TWELVE: Stand Alone (When Necessary) *81*
CHAPTER THIRTEEN: Say Something Crazy *87*
CHAPTER FOURTEEN: Be Full of Grace (and Truth) *93*
CHAPTER FIFTEEN: Relinquish Control *101*
      The Final Word: "Be Brave" 107

4 BE JESUS

CHAPTER SIXTEEN: Do I Believe What Jesus Believed? *113*

CHAPTER SEVENTEEN: Do My Words Match My Actions? *119*

CHAPTER EIGHTEEN: Do I Really Know Jesus? *123*

CHAPTER NINETEEN: Do I Do What Jesus Did? *129*

CHAPTER TWENTY: Do I Live as if Jesus Matters More Than Anything? *135*

The Final Word: "Be Jesus" 141

Epilogue: The Final, Final Word 145

Notes *153*

INTRODUCTION

I WAS LEANING OVER THE BACKYARD FENCE, talking to my neighbor, when the idea lodged itself in my brain and refused to leave.

John was raking leaves. I was raking leaves. And I'm a personable guy, so when I saw him in his backyard, I called out, "Hey, John, how ya doing?"

In the usual way of introverts everywhere, he tried pretending I wasn't there for a bit. When that didn't work, he replied with something fairly profound and pithy: "Hey."

My first instinct was, of course, to simply move on to my next backyard chore, making sure to look incredibly busy, almost as if I hadn't noticed that he hadn't really noticed me. (Yep, I'm as insecure about all this as the next guy.)

I'm not sure why, but I suppressed that instinct and barely mustered up enough courage to stroll over to our common fence. I leaned over it nonchalantly, as if I didn't have a care in the world and wasn't thinking about all the things I could be doing instead of talking to this neighbor who was clearly busier than I was and didn't want to talk to me anyway. It was a pretty darn good backyard-fence lean. I asked, "So, John, whatcha doin' there?"

He looked up, leaning on his leaf rake, and said, "Raking leaves."

Like most of my neighbors, John wondered what I did for a living. They had asked me probably hundreds of times (with tilted heads, squinty eyes, and slightly crinkled noses). Their impressions ranged from *a very important author* (okay, not really—I made that one up on their behalf) to *some kind of US spy to the Middle East*. All they knew was that I didn't have a real job. Sometimes I'd be in my PJs until noon, talking on the phone or writing on the front porch or working from my computer on our back deck. I was constantly leaving our cul-de-sac in a sudden rush or coming back home from somewhere with my little carry-on suitcase. My wife and I usually had a houseful of guests coming and going, and one of our daughters lived in Beirut. Not exactly the typical American family.

Anyway, after John said something about raking his leaves, I replied that the weather was nice, and then we talked Denver Broncos football and why the Rockies baseball team wouldn't be any good that year (again).

It was actually a fairly typical backyard across-the-fence conversation. It could have happened in the front yard while we were mowing our lawns or at our common cul-de-sac mailbox. Each of us had several of these ol' "Hey, how's it going?" conversations every day.

But what I did after I finished my conversation with John

was a little unusual. I went downstairs and e-mailed my assistant, Jesse. I asked him to start looking at every conversation Jesus had with anyone about anything. Short or long. Deep and profound or simple and menial.

You see, I do that sort of thing. Whenever I think of almost anything in any situation, I relate it back to Jesus and how he did that same thing. It's an exercise that helps me think and act like him.

Poor Jesse. I had him read every single conversation Jesus had in the Gospels, write them out, list them, read them out loud, time them, and send me all his findings. I did the same thing.

And we found that the average length of Jesus' conversations as recorded in the Gospels was 42 seconds long. Of course, he had conversations that were longer and shorter than that. And I don't think that these are necessarily the full conversations or that what's recorded is in real time, to be read out loud the way Jesse and I did. But they're all we have. These conversations provide much of what we know of Jesus and how he related to people.

That brief, normal, everyday interaction with John made me obsessed with the short conversations Jesus had. Because, Jesus being Jesus, his conversations were typically anything but normal. And when I realized this—when I realized that Jesus managed to turn otherwise everyday conversations into something more profound—I knew I had to figure out how he did it. Maybe I'd find nothing earth-shattering, but I hoped it would move me just one step more toward Jesus.

I'm hoping it just might do the same for you, too.

■　■　■

Humans are hardwired for relationship. Relationship with God. Relationship with each other. And many churches and other organized groups of Jesus followers spend a lot of time and energy preparing us to connect those two types of relationships—to create deep and important moments when we get to lead someone to Jesus or explain the Trinity or have some other deep conversation about God, spirituality, and life.

But when was the last time you had one of those conversations? While many of us might long to talk with someone about spiritual things (and some of us dread it), those opportunities don't happen very often. Being prepared for those conversations is good and important, but we often miss the fundamental first step. Talking to someone about spiritual things doesn't happen out of nowhere. Those conversations emerge out of the countless connections we make every day. Are we ready for those interactions? Or do we write them off as insignificant?

Stop and think of all the people you interacted with yesterday. And by interacted with, I mean people you exchanged words with, verbal or written. The neighbor you ran into at the mailbox; the barista who made your jumbo extra-hot mocha cappuccino with skim milk and light whipped cream; the lady in the cubicle next to yours; the customer-service rep. How many can you remember? For most of us, by the time we get to the end of a day, those quick connections are just blurs.

Our lives are full of these short interactions, but we seem to be under the impression that they're not overly significant. I'd like to challenge us to see them in a different light. After all, Jesus did.

Jesus was a master at making short interactions with people significant. And from my understanding of Scripture and my life experience, I genuinely believe that doing things the way he did them is the best way for every person in the world to live. Imitating Jesus is what it means to be his disciple, or life student. Disciples look at how Jesus lived and how he spoke with people, and they try every day to follow suit.

Contemporary Christian lingo has mistakenly, I believe, set up a dichotomy between *discipleship* and *evangelism*. Jesus had conversations all the time with those who thought they were close to God and those who deemed themselves lost and without hope. He invited all of them to come learn from him. So even though a good deal of this book has to do with helping people who are far away from Jesus follow him more closely, this is probably the last time I'll use the word *evangelism*.

This is good news for all of us. It frees us up to talk about the most important part of our lives in a way that's natural, meaningful, and helpful instead of staged, clumsy, and irrelevant. Anyone who has spent countless uncomfortable hours walking from house to house attempting to force awkward spiritual conversations knows exactly what I mean. I even moved across the world just to have frustrating conversations with the "heathen" about their wicked ways. Somewhere along the line, I realized that it didn't get me anywhere and that it didn't get the heathen anywhere either.

I think I've found a better way, one that has been right in front of us all along: using the ordinary moments of our lives the way Jesus used similar moments in his. This book isn't written with the aim of turning your barber into a pastor in 42 seconds. (He's probably better at cutting hair than giving sermons anyway.) Rather, our goal is simply for Jesus to be a natural part of our lives and everyday interactions with people.

■　■　■

So how are we going to get there? It's fairly easy. And extraordinarily difficult.

In this book, we're going to work through four sections that progress in level of difficulty and cost. Learning how to truly, simply engage with people like Jesus isn't hard. At least not at first. But it's a process. We have to learn how to engage the everyday moments in simple ways before we can enter into the profound, life-giving implications.

This is why we start with kindness. We need to remind ourselves that it's important to be kind, and we'll do that in section 1. After all, Jesus was kind to people (well, except the religious people).

Then in section 2, we'll discuss the practice of being present. In our crazy-busy world, we find it harder and harder to be fully present. So we're going to take a look at some practical ways we can be honestly and genuinely *with* the person right in front of us.

In order to have conversations like Jesus had, we need courage, which we'll talk about in section 3. We find talk of bravery and courage everywhere in present-day writing, both secular and Christian. (Brené Brown is a great example.) But we often forget that Jesus was brave, and that should propel us forward more than any inspirational quote we read. For most of us, it takes courage just to walk across the street and invite our neighbors over for a barbecue. Forget the Navy SEALs or the stuff we see in the movies—we just need to greet Sam and Beth at the mailbox.

Finally, in section 4, I encourage us to "be Jesus." To have his mind and his heart. The first three sections of this book are about interacting with people the way Jesus interacted. Learning to be like him in our everyday conversations. The fourth section takes us a little deeper, calling us to a *knowing* of Jesus that brings transformation. He promised that he would be with us, that he would be in us. When we believe that to be true, we can actually be the presence of Jesus to people as we are transformed into his likeness.

Each section has five days of reading with a central theme. I'd encourage you to study this book over the period of one month, one section per week. And ideally, read and live it in community. There's value and accountability in doing this kind of thing together. We cheer each other on. We challenge each other. We get to see Jesus doing things in each other's lives and the lives of everyone we come across. To encourage this practice of togetherness, I've included "Dig Deeper & Discuss" questions in the "Final Word" of each section. (Of course, you can go through this book on your own and still expect to benefit from it.)

We will spend most of our time looking at the life of Jesus—what he modeled for us in his short conversations. And I'll share my own stories along the way, as I've tried to live out this manner of interacting with other people. I'm going to share the great "wow" stories alongside the many times I've floundered, failed, or even royally blown it. If we're going to be serious about living in the way of Jesus, we're going to need the humility to understand that we're not always going to do it perfectly.

This journey we're about to take together will be practical and spiritually transformative if we let it. And I think we'll have some fun along the way.

It's time to learn to talk like Jesus. Are you ready?

1 Be Kind

*A single act of kindness throws out roots in all directions, and
the roots spring up and make new trees.* AMELIA EARHART

*"Let the little children come to me, and do not hinder them,
for the kingdom of God belongs to such as these." . . . And he
took the children in his arms, placed his hands on them and
blessed them.* JESUS, MARK 10:14, 16

Most of us have seen it somewhere: the painting, book
illustration, or even felt-board diagram of smiling,
laughing Jesus, surrounded by smiling, laughing children,
each trying to find their place on his lap. The image might
take us back to happy childhood Sunday school lessons. Or
perhaps we've relegated the picture to the mental category
of "overly simplistic thoughts about God." But I'd suggest
it's time to take that image out, dust it off, and revel in the
powerful and often overlooked truth that Jesus was kind.
Simply kind.

Kindness has gotten a bad rap lately. Being nice to people
sounds like you're about to have some sort of liberal kumbaya
moment or silly group hug while ignoring the less-than-kind
world around you. Because in this world of ours, being kind

doesn't have much value. That goes for many Christians, too. A *whole lot* of people who say they follow Jesus have a hair-trigger temper, ready to jump down someone's throat at the slightest disagreement or wrongdoing. We rationalize it. We justify it. I even know some Christians who say things like "Jesus wasn't nice—he was right."

Of course, in saying that, we forget that kindness is a fruit of the Spirit. It's number five on Paul's list, right after "love, joy, peace, patience."[1] It's one of the top qualities we're to exhibit if we have the Spirit of Jesus in our lives.

So that's why, if we're going to be like Jesus in our everyday interactions, we have to go back to basics. Kindness 101. Encouragement to be nice to those around us. Basic human being sort of stuff. These are the things we sometimes miss in the busyness and craziness of life. Kindness is the foundation for everything else in this book. It's basically impossible to introduce our neighbors and coworkers to Jesus if we're not kind to them.

Kindness isn't hard, but it does take lifting our heads up and noticing the people around us. It takes being willing to set our selfishness aside to think about other people. Kindness can be transformative. It can affect the person you're talking to in ways you might not even see.

And it just might change you as well.

CHAPTER ONE

Say Hey

The Nonstarter: Fail to acknowledge someone.
The Opener: Say hello. Hi. Hey. Howdy.

JESUS WAS NICE TO PEOPLE.

Read that again. Almost sounds funny, right? Jesus was many things to people, but "nice" isn't always the first one we think of. We think of the miracles, the teaching, the walk to the cross, and nice seems pretty far down the list of what was a big deal about Jesus. But he was, in fact, nice to people. I mean, he wasn't particularly kind to religious people—at least not to those who used their religion to beat people up rather than share the Good News. He was also sometimes a bit hard on wealthy people and those who thought they had some sort of inherent power. But generally, to most people, most of the time, he was a pretty nice guy.

But let's look a little closer at what "nice to people" meant according to Jesus.

Jesus incorporated greeting people into his basic theology of ministry. In both Matthew 10:12 and Luke 10:5, when he gave his disciples practical instructions on how to go out and share the Good News, he told them to greet those they interacted with. If the other person returned that greeting, the disciples were to stay and hang out there. If not, they were to say, "Yo, what's up?" (my translation) and then just keep on moving.

Here's my version of that: When I kindly say hello to someone and they say a nice hello back, then we're off and running. It's really that simple. Pastor John Wimber liked to say that 90 percent of all successful ministry was just getting out of bed in the morning. This is another version of that. You can't be effective at whatever you're trying to do if you don't say a warm hello to people. That's where it all begins.

Jesus greeted some fishermen, and they ended up giving their livelihood—and eventually their lives—to follow him.[1]

Jesus greeted the Samaritan woman at the well and asked if she could give him a drink of water. And that led to one of the most powerful and often quoted stories in all the Bible.[2]

Jesus said hi to the children along the way, and they wouldn't stop coming to him.[3]

Jesus said hey to the two guys walking on the road to Emmaus, and the next thing you know, he was eating dinner with them.[4]

It all starts with hello.

I live in a cul-de-sac, so it's theoretically easy to say hello to my neighbors. Especially at around 7:00 a.m. or 6:00 p.m. on workdays, or really any time on the weekend. But I have a garage-door opener in my car, and when I just don't feel like saying hi (knowing it might lead to a real conversation), I reach up and push that little black button of personal choice and freedom. My garage door rises like the door to my castle, and *bam*, I don't need to say hi to my neighbors.

But I try to resist that temptation. Or because it sort of makes sense to go ahead and pull my car into the garage, I'll walk back outside and say hi to whoever's around.

It looks like this. I pull the car in, then walk out front and look around until I see someone and yell, "Hey, John!" (or whatever the person's name is). That's pretty much it. They usually yell back something like "Hey, Carl, what's up?" And then we might be done. Or it might go somewhere like my asking back, "How are you doing?" And once you get to "How are you doing?" you'd better watch out, because every once in a while, people actually say how they're doing.

This week make the time to say hi to people. Everywhere. Almost always. Go out of your way, look them in the eye, and say hello. Often add the ever-so-dangerous "How are you?" And try to actually mean it—like Jesus did.

Just see what happens.

CHAPTER TWO

Acknowledge the Waiter

The Nonstarter: Ignore those the world considers unimportant.
The Opener: Look them in the eye. Pay attention. Greet them.

JESUS ACKNOWLEDGED PEOPLE. Particularly those whom others didn't care about. Children. The poor. Women. Samaritans. Lepers. Dead people. Pretty much everyone.

Of all the things I love about Jesus, this is one of my favorites. He wasn't too cool for anyone. Sometimes I think I am, but Jesus—even though he was divinity with flesh—didn't act too big for his sandals.

Jesus paid attention.

To the blind beggar. When the disciples told him to move on, he stopped instead.

To the poor. The hungry. The children. The disciples (me) would typically try to keep Jesus focused—on mission. But he seemed happy to be interrupted.

Matthew, Mark, and Luke tell my favorite of these interruption stories in just a handful of verses.[1] Jesus was approached by a very important man. Matthew calls him "a ruler."[2] Mark tells us more: that his name was Jairus and he was the ruler of a synagogue.[3] Jairus had a daughter who was dying, and he asked Jesus to come to his house and heal her.

Now, think about this for a second. The man who came to Jesus was a very important religious leader. Some have speculated that he was the patron or financial backer of that Galilean synagogue. Sort of like the CEO. And if Jesus needed anything at that time in his ministry, it was some love from the local Jewish leaders. (Jesus had done some things to make the religious leaders pretty upset: hanging out with sinners, breaking religious food laws, challenging their hypocrisy.) And now standing before him was a Jewish leader who actually had faith in him. Jairus believed that Jesus could, and would, heal his daughter. Pretty remarkable, given the tensions between Jesus and the religious establishment.

This was Jesus' chance. If he did a miracle for Jairus, he could get on the religious leaders' good sides again.

Jesus agreed to go with Jairus, but on the way, he was interrupted by an extremely inappropriate lady. She pushed her way through the crowd and touched him while she was bleeding and religiously unclean. All wrong.

Let me interrupt the story with an honest moment. Sometimes after I've spoken at an event and somehow said something good or helpful, a small crowd will form around me (not like Jesus' crowds—more like a crowd of four). And more often than not, someone will walk right past those four as if they didn't exist and start talking to me. That really, really annoys me.

Or maybe I'm signing books after a talk and someone cuts right to the front of the line for no apparent reason, as if they're blind.

I don't like rude people. And it's even worse if they're inappropriate in some cultural sense. Sometimes I tell them that they're rude, or I just ignore them.

But, well, not Jesus.

He stopped for the interruption. He asked who touched him. He took time, in front of everybody, to talk to the socially unacceptable lady. And what I love most about this story is that he instantly healed her.

Actually, she was healed before Jesus even spoke to her, right as she'd reached out and touched the hem of his robe. The power to heal went out from him right away, but he still took the time to have a conversation.

Jesus allowed himself to be interrupted as he was traveling to see Jairus's dying daughter. And you know what happened? Luke tells us that "while he was still speaking to her,"[4] the report came that Jairus's daughter had died. So there was no need for Jesus to come.

Imagine. Let me put it in context. Let's say the mayor of Denver had personally come to me and asked if I'd go pray for his daughter. The press was there. This would be the biggest moment of my life. Of course, in deep spiritual humility I had said yes.

And on the way, a beggar on the streets of downtown grabbed my pant leg and asked for money.

Would I have stopped? And talked to him? And given him what he asked for?

I don't think I'll answer!

But Jesus did. He allowed an unknown woman of questionable credentials to interrupt him in the middle of his most important appearance to date.

The juxtaposition couldn't be more obvious: a prominent male religious synagogue ruler on the one side, and an unknown, religiously unclean woman on the other. When we know Jesus, we shouldn't be surprised that he stopped for her. But it sure was a surprise to everyone at the time.

I can only imagine the disciples' indignation upon hearing the news that the important man's little girl had died. "If only Jesus hadn't stopped," they must have said. But when Jesus heard the news, he turned to Jairus and said, "Don't be afraid."[5] Jesus gives the number one command in all the Bible: Don't fear. Because I'm sure Jairus was, as we all so often are, afraid.

We know the end of the story. Both the bleeding woman and the important man's daughter were healed. The normal order of things was upended. Jesus chose to give as much attention to the social outcast as he did to the religious man; he stopped to talk to the lesser-known person rather than give precedence to the well known.

Jesus almost always did that.

We should too.

Living in Beirut, Lebanon, for twelve years provided me and my wife, Chris, with ample opportunity to acknowledge the less fortunate. We passed beggars every day on the street.

They were sometimes friendly and other times obnoxious. But we made a decision: We would look at each one and smile. Yep, that's it. I feel foolish even writing that sentence. Because we didn't give them all money; we didn't pray for them all to be healed (although we did do both of those things sometimes). But still I try to always look a beggar in the eye.

Yes, doing that invites more begging. I constantly hear that looking at or engaging them in any way only encourages them to keep begging. Probably true. Oh well. It's good for me to do it. I think it at least reminds me that they are as human as I am. And maybe it reminds them of the same. It's pretty easy for us to both dehumanize the other. Do you think that beggars see us as human, or as a source to get something from? They may be ignoring our humanity, just as we might try to ignore theirs. Simple eye contact, a smile, and a hello might do more than we think.

There was a man in a wheelchair named Zachariah on our street in downtown West Beirut. He was there for years. He was paralyzed from the waist down and had burn marks all over his body. We became friends. Actual friends. He would be begging—looking very sad and sorry, holding out his hand—and then see us and stop begging and break out into a huge smile. He'd call our names and we'd stop to chat. He was awesome. Sometimes we'd try to give him money and he'd refuse. He told us he didn't want money from his friends.

One day our daughter Marie, without our even knowing, emptied her piggy bank and brought out a bag of money. I'd guess it was about twenty dollars' worth of Lebanese coins.

She wanted to give it to Zachariah. She did. He cried. We cried. He couldn't say no to this precious gift even though he didn't want to take it. That's hope. A small dose of the gospel. A widow's mite. An alabaster jar of perfume. A sweet-smelling sacrifice of both time and money and, perhaps more important, also of dignity. What's worth more? Our acknowledging his friendship and humanity to the point where even our own daughter would give all her money, or his begging and someone giving him a thousand dollars?

This week let's try to acknowledge those we don't normally pay much attention to. Let's make eye contact with beggars even if we don't always give them money. Let's acknowledge those who are serving us. The waitstaff at a restaurant. Even when you're having a world-changing conversation with your friend. Stop when the busboy comes up to refill your water and just look him in the eye and say, "Thank you so much." See what it does.

CHAPTER THREE

Ask Another Question

The Nonstarter: Be quick to give answers.
The Opener: Ask one more question.

JESUS DIDN'T ANSWER very many questions. It's almost funny. He either replied with a better question—even one that seemingly had no relation to the original question—or with a story that didn't always make a whole lot of sense (we call them "parables"). Think about that for a while. Jesus almost never did what we almost always do: give a direct answer.

I was taught from an early age to answer when asked, whether it was a direct or indirect question. Reply when spoken to. I was taught that to be smart meant to know the answers. And that the only way someone else would know I was smart would be if I gave "the answer."

But Jesus didn't do that. Many scholars think that he

perfected the Socratic method, which uses questions in order to arrive at a certain understanding. But that's actually not at all what he did.

Jesus used questions to actually know the people in front of him and to help them know themselves. He cared enough for others to bypass the temptation to know it all and look smart, in order to actually draw people out.

Think of some of Jesus' great questions:

"Do you want to get well?"[1]

"What do you want me to do for you?"[2]

"Do you love me?"[3]

"Who is my mother, and who are my brothers?"[4]

"Where are your accusers?"[5]

"Who do you say I am?"[6]

I love this last one. Instead of Jesus clearly explaining to the disciples who he was (like I would try to do), he asked them who they thought he was. And this was after they'd been with him for at least two full years!

Here's what I would have imagined Jesus doing much earlier on in his earthly career. He should have gathered the Twelve around him and said something like this:

> Okay, guys, here's the deal. I know you've been wondering about my true identity. Talking about me behind my back. So here's the thing: I'm God. In the flesh. Later, people will call it the Incarnation. Fully God. Fully man. Hate to say it, but some who claim to follow me will even kill each other over this point. I digress. I know that my dad's name is Joseph and

my mom is Mary, but actually, well . . . I'm God.
And I know this is a shocker, but I'm gonna let those
Romans kill me in another year or so. I don't know
the exact time, because only my Father knows that
part. Yep, I'm his Son, but he still knows some stuff
I don't know.

Anyhoo, Peter, are you paying attention? It looks
like you're daydreaming.

Then after I die, I will rise again. I'll have a new
body, but it will be different. And then I'll go back
where I came from, to live with my Father. And I'll
still be with you, but in a different kind of way. I'll
explain more about that later. All clear for now?

The point I'm trying to make is that Jesus didn't give the
disciples all the answers right away.

He gave lots of hints, for sure. I liken it to a jigsaw puzzle.
Or a treasure hunt.

You know what this is called? Relationship. Friendship.
Life. It's how everything else works. There is nothing in life
that we know all at once. Conversation leads to relationship;
a lecture, not so much.

I have been married to my wonderful, darling, fun wife,
Chris, a cool thirty years at the writing of this book, and I
find out things about her all the time that I didn't know.
Think of how weird it would have been if she and I were
given a divine download when we first met so we knew everything about each other. It'd be bizarre, right? But we sort of
think that coming to Jesus should be like that. I don't know

about you, but "all things being new"[7] is taking up quite a lot of time in my life. And the process of being "born again"[8] sure isn't instantaneous.

All this to say, Jesus didn't feel obligated to answer or explain everything to everyone. Or maybe not anything to anyone. Interesting how secure he was.

I talk about this point a lot when I give my little speeches and preaches at churches and such. About how Jesus never answered questions but asked better questions or told a funny story. And I do that too sometimes. But often I just answer the question. It's easier. Much less work to answer than to think of a better question. Or to wait a second and try to discern the heart behind the question.

When someone asks me why there's suffering in the world, I answer, "Because of a broken, fallen world. Sin. Original sin."

But was that really their question? Maybe that person is really asking why they've had to suffer so much. Or if God really gives a rip about all the evil that's going on in the world.

There are possibly a hundred deep questions full of mystery that I've been trained to "know" the answers to. We call this approach apologetics. It's rational, logical, and Western styled in its analytical approach to life's great questions. It's not a bad approach. It's just not the way of Jesus. Being kind like Jesus means caring enough to learn why a given question matters to an individual. Which usually means asking another question, and another, and another, and listening. But—and this is important—we don't listen just to be able to give a right answer. We listen to show that our concern goes deeper than the question itself.

Question asking feels like a lost art. I think we call it "good conversation." It could be as simple as this dialogue:

ME: Hey there. I'm Carl. What's your name?

MY NEW COWORKER, BOB: Bob. Nice to meet you, Carl.

ME: So where did you move here from?

BOB: Miami.

ME: Very cool. Nice city. Well, I haven't actually been there, but I've seen *Miami Vice* a few times.

BOB: Ha ha. (He doesn't think it's all that funny.)

ME: And do you have family?

BOB: Yep, a wife and a couple of kids.

ME: Me too. A wife and three kids. How did they feel about moving to Denver?

BOB: My wife and youngest boy were good with it. But the older one, well, not so much.

ME: Oh man, I totally get that. We've moved a few times and it was always harder on the oldest one. So what did you do before you came to join us here?

BOB: Similar work. Construction.

ME: Do you like your work?

Anyway, you get the idea. Keep asking questions. Start your questions with *who*, *what*, *when*, *where*, *why*, or *how*. Go one question deeper by asking, "What was that like for you?" Ask questions about their emotions: "How did that feel?" If I ask you, "Were you afraid?" you're going to respond to the most powerful word in that sentence: "Yes, I was very afraid." Questions let people describe their experience.

Know when to stop. Don't pry. Don't interrogate.

I have a friend who tends to dive in too deep too quickly. Within two minutes, he's asking the person about the health of their marriage. Although some may find this inviting, many are put off by it. Just let the conversation unfold naturally. Pause. Take a breath. Let there be more give and take. Let them ask you as many questions as you're asking them. But always try to go one question deeper.

When you ask what they do and they say, "I'm an engineer," it might be tempting to say, "Oh cool," and leave it at that. But that's no fun. What kind of engineer? What kind of projects are her favorite to work on? Why? It takes some energy and thought, but it's well worth it—if you care about people. And we do. Right?

This week what we're going to try to do is not answer, as odd as that may sound. Okay, so if someone asks you directions to the grocery store and you know, go ahead and tell them. But when people ask you life questions, big questions, spiritual questions, just try not answering. At least not directly. You might "answer" them by asking, "Well, what do you think?" Or you can ask them to clarify: "That's a great question. Tell me more. I want to be sure I have it." Or "I'm not sure I fully understand and I don't want to say something without thinking it through. Can you tell me more?" These are simple yet effective tools to having a deeper and more meaningful conversation. And one that leads somewhere that's helpful and productive.

By the way, I don't think these conversations need to "lead somewhere"—like we're trying to get them to believe in something or to change somehow. I just mean that our exchange leads to better understanding of one another and a more substantive relationship. Maybe we could even say that this kind of conversation helps us be more fully human. To really know others and to allow ourselves to be known. All of us yearn for someone to care enough to ask us good, deep questions that will draw out the best from within us.

Let's be those people! Let's try it.

CHAPTER FOUR

Do Something Small

The Nonstarter: Watch your elderly neighbor shovel snow.
The Opener: Mow your neighbor's yard for no reason.

JESUS SERVED PEOPLE. It's hard to argue that simple point. He came to serve, not to be served. *Suffering servant* was even a title given to him in the Hebrew Scriptures.[1]

Jesus served people in simple but powerful ways: healing a blind man by simply acknowledging his faith, cleansing a leper with a touch, or driving out a demon with a word. So it's a little challenging to translate from his life to our own.

However, I take great comfort in the set of short parables from Matthew 13. Each parable is about a hidden thing: a mustard seed in the ground, yeast in a lump of dough, a hidden treasure, a pearl in an oyster shell. And each one teaches us that the Kingdom starts small.

Each of these things is insignificant in its own right.

A mustard seed is very small; to become a tree, it has to be buried.

Yeast on its own does nothing; it only has visible effect when mixed into dough.

Treasure that's buried isn't worth anything.

A pearl inside an oyster is at the bottom of the sea.

Small things that may seem insignificant have always been the keys to Jesus' Kingdom.

Jesus turns everything upside down and inside out. Some who are not known now will later be known. Many working behind the scenes will gain the greatest rewards. Death brings life. You have to lose your life in order to find it. The ones who the world thinks are "leaders" might actually not be, and others who are simple servants might be honored for their significant impact.

I have a hard time with this one. I believe it, I'm writing it, but it's hard for me to practice. I'm usually very impressed with "leaders." I like the smell of success. I want to be around it, and I want to have it. I love a church, organization, or company that's cool in the world's eyes.

I want to do business with winners—no losers in the circle. I want to be around strong, powerful leaders who are doing things I consider significant. And I want to be like them.

But Jesus sure spent a lot of time with what we might call "small players." He constantly ran from the praise of people. He sometimes drew big crowds, but he never encouraged them. In fact, he often escaped to quiet places away from the crowds. It seems like he was fairly hard on people we would consider influential—the rich people, the religious leaders of the day—and overly kind to and admiring of the "small" people of the world—the widow who gave just two mites, the Canaanite mother whose daughter was possessed by a demon, the blind beggar.[2]

My wife, Chris, is better at so many of these things than I am. She's never scheming or planning for the next thing; she's just present, loving whoever is in front of her. She lives in the moment and is kind to everyone she meets. She's my example of this way of living like Jesus.

Many years ago, she decided to do a kids' club in Beirut. It was going to be a weeklong, four-hour-a-day summer camp. She started with our three kids and their friends.

Chris gathered a team to help. She was okay with the small number of kids, but I was frustrated and didn't even want to move ahead. (I equated "small" with "insignificant," I'm embarrassed to say.)

One of the young Lebanese university students and his girlfriend, also a university student, were helping us and had an idea. Why not go out on the streets and collect street kids to come? These were the total outcasts of society, and no one liked them. The university student was the son of an influential and wealthy leader in the country, and I couldn't believe that he would even have such an idea.

We weren't sure the "outcasts" would come. We also wondered if the owners of the building would stop them from coming in. We weren't convinced that our three kids and their other four friends would like sharing their time with these dirty, disorderly street kids. And we didn't know if we could manage them if they did come.

That's a lot of ifs. But we said, "Okay. Let's try."

So these two young university students went looking for street kids to join us. They came back in about two hours and said, "Yep, they want to come. They will be here tomorrow morning at nine."

And sure enough, by about eight thirty the next day, there was a whole pile of kids we didn't know. A few we recognized, but most were just dirty, smelly street kids. About ten of them. And they came every day that week—and loved it. And our kids and their friends included them just like they were one of us. We were so proud.

From that time, we began a weekly ministry to these street kids. They'd come at least once every week for tutoring, Bible stories, fun, and games. Our young university students led them in almost every way. Some of these kids even found ultimate life as they encountered Jesus.

Anna, our twenty-five-year-old daughter, now lives in Beirut, working and ministering there. Last month she was walking down the street close to the same building that hosted these kids, when a woman came up and asked, "Are you Anna, Chris and Carl's daughter?"

Anna said she was. This lady, Mariam, was the university student who, with her boyfriend, had decided to go out and invite the street kids. She is now married with five kids of her own, still living in Beirut.

She said she just wanted to encourage Anna because she found out Anna was working with Syrian refugee kids. Many of the street kids we'd worked with had been Syrian as well.

Then Mariam told Anna this story. The week before,

a young man in his midtwenties came up to her on the street and said, "Miss Mariam, do you remember me?" She didn't but asked him to continue.

The young man proceeded to say, "Twenty years ago, I was a five-year-old street kid who came to your kids' club. As I came each week, you taught me about life and Jesus. I now am a believer and follow Jesus and have been admitted into a university in Canada. I just wanted you to know that you changed my life."

Mariam said to our daughter Anna, "What you're doing now with these Syrian refugee kids will change their lives. Don't give up."

Jesus' Kingdom starts with small things!

This week I wonder if we could do a few small things.

Be kind to a stranger.

Give the homeless person with the sign on the street five dollars and tell him you'll pray for him—and actually pray for him.

Mow your neighbor's yard for no reason.

Pay for the groceries of the person behind you in line or the coffee of the next person up at Starbucks. Buy lunch for the people at the table next to yours.

Tell those people that God loves them.

These are not just silly "random acts of kindness" for no reason. You're doing these things because God values small things. Who knows what it might lead to?

CHAPTER FIVE

Talk to the Kid

The Nonstarter: Ignore your friends' children.
The Opener: Get down on the floor and play with the kids.

AS I MENTIONED EARLIER. Jesus liked kids. He wanted them around. Matthew, Mark, and Luke all record the time when the crowds were bringing their children to Jesus so that he could lay his hands on them and bless them. And all three Gospels note that the disciples "rebuked" the parents for doing so.[1]

It'd be funny if it weren't so sad. Imagine. The holier-than-thou closest followers of Jesus thought he had more important things to do. *He's got to be preaching. He can't be rolling around on the grassy hillside with a bunch of grimy munchkins.*

Oh my. Embarrassing. I would never think anything like that. I mean, except for the fact that just in the previous chapter, I was ready to shut down the kids' club before it even got started. But other than that.

In Luke 18:17, Jesus said that if we don't become like a little child, we cannot enter his Kingdom. This was his response to the disciples. He went on to say that "whoever receives one such child" receives him.[2] The insinuation was not even veiled: If you don't receive a child, you are not receiving Jesus.

So I don't know about you, but it makes me want to go find some young'uns to hang out with.

But I often find myself thinking that I'm pretty important. Here's a list of people who, over the years, I thought God wanted me to focus on

- Muslims;
- leaders;
- Arabs;
- Palestinians;
- cultural influencers; and
- pastors.

Not sure if you noticed, but kids aren't on that list. Gee whiz, that's embarrassing to write out.

Okay, you are probably thinking right now that there must surely be a place for helpful focus. Boundaries. And strategic mission. And I'd say, "Maybe." I doubt there's as much of that as we like to think in our Western, goal-oriented culture, but yes, surely some. But none that excludes the kids.

Actually, if you are thinking, *I wonder what a good way would be to encourage my pastor or the leader of a country*, you might want to start with blessing their children. I know that if you want to win my heart, you pay attention to my kids.

And I'm telling you, kids have an incredible built-in BS-o-meter. They can tell if you really give a rip about them or not. While our children were growing up, we had tons of people from all over the world come through our place. And our kids figured out really quickly who they wanted to hang out with, who they wanted us to invite back, and who they didn't want around.

So many friends would come to our home and greet our kids with something like "Oh, hi. And tell me"—in a silly, condescending voice—"what's your name?" often with a pat on the head.

Then there were the ones who almost ignored Chris and me and got down on the floor with our kids. Do you think that ever upset us? No way. We loved it. Our kids loved it. We wanted our friends to know our kids. We've always wanted our kids to know our friends.

And I can tell you that all our best friends love our kids, and our kids love them.

A powerful reminder of this idea of focusing on children came just a few weeks ago in Rome when Chris and I and a couple of friends from the Middle East had the chance to meet the pope and spend about three minutes with him. I was surely the least important person in his lineup that day. There were cardinals from around the world, some heads of state, and who knows who else. So it wasn't like he woke up that morning thinking anything like *Oh boy, today I get to meet Carl. I've heard he's sort of a big deal.* Nope.

But before he came to meet the others who may have actually been big deals, he took a *long* time—frankly, an annoyingly long time—to greet kids in the crowd. Random children. He talked to them. Got out of his fairly cool popemobile and walked among them. Held them. He didn't give much time to their parents, but man, did he ever focus on the kids. It seemed to bring him joy.

So here's the challenge. Take a moment to scroll through the list of your closest friends. Do you know their kids? By name? Their interests? Do you buy them birthday gifts? When you talk to your friends, do you ask about their kids—and really listen?

What about your neighbors? Do you know their kids' names and where they go to school and what their favorite classes are? If not, all it takes is a little time. If you want to reach someone's heart, love their kids.

The Final Word: "Be Kind"

BEING KIND ISN'T HARD. Well, maybe it is. We're naturally self-focused, and kindness means moving beyond that, means setting our own priorities aside to think about someone else and treat them the way we want to be treated. But it shouldn't be difficult. It should be the natural rhythm of every life. I don't think I know anyone who would disagree with that. Jesus certainly wouldn't.

So be kind. Nice. Friendly. Greet people. Look them in the eye. Ask another question. Acknowledge the beggars, the servers, and those who inhabit the "background." Laugh with a child. Act in these kind ways of Jesus until his ways become yours. I expect you'll be surprised by the joy you discover and the open doors you'll have for sharing more of Jesus' Good News.

DIG DEEPER & DISCUSS

1. Reflect upon a time when someone's simple kindness had a larger-than-visible impact on your life.

2. Read some of the Scripture passages referenced in this section (Matthew 13; 15:22-28; Mark 10:13-14;

Luke 8:40-48; 18:35-43; 21:1-4; John 4:1-26). What story or conversation of Jesus most demonstrates his kindness?

3. This week we were challenged to show kindness in intentional ways. Which of the following did you attempt? How did it go?

a. Go out of your way to look people in the eye and say hello.

b. Acknowledge the people you normally fail to recognize.

c. Refrain from giving answers and ask another question.

d. Do a small act of kindness or thoughtfulness for someone. Just because.

e. Get to know the kids of some of your friends and neighbors. Ask a question about them. Learn their names. Show that you see and value them.

2 Be Present

God is always coming to you in the Sacrament of the Present Moment. Meet and receive Him there with gratitude in that sacrament. EVELYN UNDERHILL

As Jesus and his disciples were on their way, he came to a village where a woman named Martha opened her home to him. She had a sister called Mary, who sat at the Lord's feet listening to what he said. But Martha was distracted by all the preparations that had to be made. She came to him and asked, "Lord, don't you care that my sister has left me to do the work by myself? Tell her to help me!"

"Martha, Martha," the Lord answered, "you are worried and upset about many things, but few things are needed—or indeed only one. Mary has chosen what is better, and it will not be taken away from her." LUKE 10:38-42

I have a love-hate relationship with this story. Poor Martha! Unfairly left with all the work. Would Jesus have been so quick to praise Mary if the house were dirty and lunch unmade? Hard work isn't bad, is it? Absolutely not. But it seems that Jesus, as he often did, was speaking to the deeper state of Martha's heart. She was worried and upset about many things and, in so doing, missed the actual presence of God in front of her. Mary, on the other hand, listened to what Jesus said and ultimately chose what was better: being present to what God was doing in that moment.

I read Brother Lawrence's classic, *The Practice of the Presence of God*, when I was in YWAM at age twenty. It changed me. It's basically the story of a would-be famous monk who got "stuck" washing dishes in the monastery kitchen for most of his life and how he learned to dramatically "practice" the presence of God there (proof that hard work doesn't necessarily block the ability to be present to God and others). Stunning. If you haven't read it, I'd say to put this book down and read that one.

Being present for God may be the key to life. To everything. Simply being with him, no matter where we are or what we're doing, changes us. If we don't know how to do that, all the rest doesn't matter.

I have also found that being fully present for and with people changes everything. Have you ever been speaking to someone who keeps looking over your shoulder at the next person they want to talk to? Isn't that just the worst?

But what about the person who listens intently to your stories? Who remembers to ask you about something from a conversation a few months back? Who isn't in a rush to check their phone or talk to someone else or leave? Makes you feel valued, right?

Being present is a simple practice, but it will change how you relate to the world in profound ways.

CHAPTER SIX

Breathe Deep

Nonstarter: Become an expert multitasker.
Opener: Stop. Look. See.

JESUS WAS SO MANY THINGS, some of them controversial. But one thing that was perfectly clear about his life was he was fully present in the moment. He gave people the most valuable gift of all: himself. He didn't get distracted from who was at hand because he had something better to do (like save the world).

I already noted one such example: the woman who "interrupted" him on his way to heal the ruler's dying daughter. The life of Jesus is marked by a constant sense of approachability and focus on the individual. We see this in God's character throughout the rest of Scripture as well.

To explore this further, let's take a look at the Old Testament—specifically, the book of beginnings, Genesis.

We're going to peer into the life of Abraham's maidservant, Hagar.[1]

You're probably familiar with the story. It's a classic. God promises to make Abraham the father of a great nation. But Abraham and his wife Sarai were childless. They agreed Abraham should take their Egyptian servant girl, Hagar, as a second wife so they could perhaps have a son—you know, to sort of help God out with his promise. So this Egyptian servant became pregnant with Abraham's first child, Ishmael.

Because Hagar, the new wife, was about to bear the great patriarch's first kid, she started to act a little more important than she should have. So (not surprisingly) Sarai started to intensely dislike her and complained to Abraham. She started harassing Hagar. The pregnant Hagar fled, and while she sat beside the road, trying to figure out what to do and where to go, "the angel of the Lord" spoke to her. They had quite a conversation, actually, ending with the spectacular promise of God for the descendants of Ishmael.[2]

But here's the cool thing that you might not have noticed. God saw her. Some scholars would say that "the angel of the Lord" was an appearance of the preincarnate Christ. And I love his question to Hagar: "Where have you come from and where are you going?"[3] Wow.

He proclaims a blessing over her and her descendants. And then—get ready for this—she gives God a name. She says, "You are the God who sees me."[4] *El Roi.*

Hagar, the Egyptian, made this discovery. *This god is the God who sees. Me. Not the tribe. Not the clan. Me.*

She had the chutzpah to name God. More than a bit

audacious. But she must have felt so personally touched that she did it with confidence.

Hagar understood what the writers and artists and philosophers of the Renaissance would "discover" in the fourteenth and fifteenth centuries in Europe. That the individual human matters. It's what Martin Luther (re)discovered in the sixteenth century in Germany. That our God is a personal God. He knows us and wants to be known by us. We can have a personal friendship with this God. He is not far away. He is actually our closest friend.

Nearly four thousand years before the cultural Renaissance and spiritual Reformation, this Egyptian servant spoke this truth aloud. A personal deity who "sees people" was unheard of. Imagine. God looked down and saw her. Noticed. Cared. And asked a very personal question about where she'd come from and where she was going.

Hagar took the question literally, though my guess is that the angel of the Lord meant it more deeply than she took it. He probably cared less about her physical destination than about her spiritual identity.

She exclaimed with great joy that she had "now seen the One who sees me,"[5] and things would never be the same again. She had been seen by the Almighty.

This is the same God who ultimately sees us. He became one of us. He was born like us. He breathed our air and ate and drank like us. He felt our pain and shared our suffering. He experienced death. He then rose again, as we who follow him will one day do!

Jesus looked deeply into the eyes of the hurting and the

lost and asked them where they were coming from and where they were going. And he wants to walk with us on that journey. Jesus has always been there and will always be here—with us.

And in this example, we find how we're supposed to be as well. This God, represented most fully and perfectly in Jesus from Nazareth, has laid before us an example of perfect presence. If we are going to be like Jesus, we need to offer people the gift of being 100 percent present in our everyday conversations. Doing that will change us—and maybe our world.

Let me tell you, I'm not always good at this. I get busy. I ignore people. The great irony is that as I wrote this chapter, I literally ignored three people who were here at my house. (Do I get credit for at least acknowledging I was being a jerk?)

It's sometimes hard for me to slow down and focus on who's in front of me. Taking a deep breath and relaxing is not my strong suit. I'm one of those nutty people who likes the feeling of chaos, who thrives on the edge of out of control. Most people use the phrase *juggling too many plates* as a negative, but I welcome the opportunity to grab one more plate just to show you I can do it. I like new challenges. I'm a good multitasker. A dreamer. An entrepreneur.

These are personality traits and gifts, but they can't be my excuse for failing to see and be present with the person in front of me.

When I was growing up, I was very self-dependent, and I spent a lot of time alone, not caring too much what other people thought or were doing. I would go by myself on survival backpacking trips for up to two weeks at a time, just living off the land with my dog, my gun, my fishing line, and some matches to start a fire. On family vacations, I'd get up at daybreak and go fishing by myself, often not coming back until dark.

But my story is one full of God changing me. And this aspect of my life changed, literally, in one day.

I was nineteen years old and living on my own. My parents and two sisters had moved to Albuquerque, and I stayed behind in Colorado Springs to work. I had my own apartment, my own car, and my own money. And for the first time, I got to choose my own church. Because I grew up as a pastor's kid, I'd never had the opportunity before. And you know what I did? I chose an Assemblies of God church, the same kind my dad had pastored most of my life. But it was still new for me.

And that was the day. The day I decided to change. I formulated this thought: *Everyone here will be insecure, just like I am. I should pretend to be outgoing, fun, and interesting since no one will know anyway.*

So I did. And *bam*—instant results. My hypothesis was correct. When I acted like I wasn't insecure, everyone else thought I was cool. I even ended up starting and leading the whole singles' group at this large church. I met my future wife, Chris, there. We led the group together for quite some time.

Just like that, I was outgoing. A leader. Successful. Pretty nifty, eh?

Then people around me started telling me that I was going to lead "big things." And I became an evangelist.

A missionary. A church planter. All according to expectation. Pleasing others. Proving I'm somebody.

I've lived out of that place for most of my life.

But here's the problem: Being outgoing, being an evangelist or church planter, didn't automatically make me more present. In fact, it often made me the opposite. If I was leading people, then I needed to be out in front, or on the mountaintop, hearing from God. I was, by definition of the role (or what I thought was the definition of the role), separated from them.

So I've been on a journey of reconnecting with God and people. Rather than living out someone else's expectations for me, which then became my own, I've been asking God to restore the beautiful balance of being alone so that when I'm with people, I have something of substance to give. When I see someone, I want to be excited that there's another human standing right there in front of me. Imagine the possibilities.

So what if this week we all agree to practice the present of presence? Let's fully give ourselves to those we meet. No multitasking. When we're in a conversation and find ourselves thinking about what we're going to have for dinner, let's either pull ourselves back into the present or pull ourselves out of the conversation. One or the other. Just don't leave people feeling like they don't matter because you can't be fully with them in the moment.

If you want to be intentionally present with people, try asking two questions: Where have you come from, and where are you going?

Then listen. God gave us two ears and one mouth. Use

them in proportion. We have a hard time listening rather than talking because, well, we'd rather talk. Talking keeps us in control. We don't have to hear anything we're not interested in. We're the center of attention. We can bolster our own identities. Try listening to understand, not to formulate your reply.

If you need quiet time, go somewhere alone. If you find yourself (as I often do) too tired to be fully present with those you meet, that means you need to recharge your battery. So go and do that. Then come back into the game of life fully recharged, ready to see others for who they really are.

CHAPTER SEVEN

Stop Trying to Be Cool

Nonstarter: Try to impress.
Opener: Be vulnerable.

JESUS REALLY WASN'T ALL THAT COOL. By all accounts, he wasn't particularly good-looking. In fact, if you take Isaiah's prophetic mention literally, he was homely. He didn't have a good reputation. Most likely he wasn't popular with the cool kids. The rich, famous, powerful, religious, political leaders were not his best friends. Instead, they were the ones who crucified him.

And sure, although Jesus liked a good party (after all, he's the one who made dozens of bottles of the best wine), he could also be the buzzkill. He sometimes called out a host for some sin. He wasn't much for sucking up to the "in" crowd. And he seemed to purposefully spend time with the ones who could give him no favors or material support.

Plus, Jesus hid from crowds. When they caught him, he ministered to them without concern for himself, but he never sought the attention. He walked away when they tried to make him king. Jesus often and quite intentionally rejected the praise and adoration of people. He rejected Satan's temptation to shortcut suffering for the kingdoms of this world. When he sensed that people were becoming overly enamored with him, he'd deflect their praises and point them to the Father.

Perhaps my favorite passage about this is in Luke 4:18. Jesus read from the parchment of Israel's favorite prophet, Isaiah—the part where Isaiah prophesied that Jesus would be the one to "proclaim good news to the poor . . . freedom for the prisoners . . . recovery of sight for the blind . . . [and] set the oppressed free [and] proclaim the year of the Lord's favor."

The crowd just loved this. Here was a new young potential rabbi who obviously had some juice, preaching from their favorite prophet and telling them they were about to experience all these wonderful things. Lots of amens and hallelujahs to that.

Luke wryly noted, "All spoke well of him and marveled at the gracious words that were coming from his mouth."[1] The crowd liked this young man from their region. From their tribe and tongue and religion. "What a nice young man," the Jewish mothers were surely whispering amongst themselves. Maybe he'd marry one of their daughters.

Have you noticed what Jesus did next? Remember, he was certainly fully aware of the situation. It was his graduation party. His mission statement. The moment he'd been born for—to let the people of Israel know that the Messiah had come.

But no. Jesus, being Jesus, did the unexpected. Like any good preacher, he gave two examples to illustrate his point. But these were ones his audience didn't want to hear.

The first highlighted the ministry of their most loved prophet of power, Elijah. The one who killed all those nasty prophets of the false god Baal. So far so good.

"Were there no widows in Israel at the time of Elijah?"[2] he asked. The people listening likely looked around, wondering why he was even asking, since everyone knew there were widows in Israel during Elijah's time.

And then he continued, "But Elijah was not sent to them, but to a widow in Zarephath."[3] Zarephath is in what's now southern Lebanon. Controlled by Assyria at the time. Bad. The enemy.

Why was he bringing that up?

But he quickly moved right into his next sentence. This time he didn't ask—he just stated. "There were lepers in Israel in the time of Elisha, yet none of them were healed. Only Naaman the Syrian."[4] Bad. The enemy. Again.

Ouch.

Jesus used a Lebanese and a Syrian—Israel's enemies—as his examples of how Isaiah 61 was being fulfilled. In a Jewish synagogue?

There's so much to unpack in this story, but one thing that has continually struck me is how little the politics of the region have changed over the last two thousand years.

This same sermon would not work well today in a Jewish synagogue. (By the way, lest we become indignant toward one side or the other, I'm fairly certain that if Jesus had been giving that talk in a Phoenician or Assyrian temple, he would have turned the tables appropriately the other way.)

So of course the crowd did what crowds do. In a matter of minutes, they switched from loving him to wanting to kill him.

Crowds shift with the winds. Why waste the time and energy trying to be in with the popular crowd? Jesus never did. Be like him. Don't try to be cool.

Remember when I met the pope? Great guy. We had a good talk. As you might guess, we talked about the Middle East, about Muslims, and a good bit about Jesus.

Here's the deal. I could choose to leave it right there. Just letting you know that the pope and I are tight. You'd be duly impressed.

Or I could tell the rest of the story. I met him as one of a long line of people shaking his hand that day. I had about forty seconds with him. I did manage to get in something about the Middle East and how God loves Muslims. I thanked him for his love for all people, and I let him know that I'm a follower of Jesus who lives part time in Dubai with my wife (who was standing behind me in the crowd and didn't get to shake the pope's hand). So it was still an honor, for sure. He listened, nodded his head, smiled a lot, and said "Please pray for me" at the end of my spiel.

But all that's to say, I'm not expecting a call from the papal office to meet Francis for a tall cold one any time soon.

Was it "cool" for me to meet the pope? Of course. But years ago, I would have made the meeting to be much more than was real. The real part is that I did, in fact, meet him. The rest of the story is that he wouldn't know me or my name from Adam. And it's important for me, in trying to be a little like Jesus, to consciously deflect and even outright reject the potential praise of men. And I do try!

Honesty and intentional humility can also be called vulnerability. Vulnerability, basically, means "open to attack."[5] And in this world of ours, nothing opens us up to attack quite like owning who we really are. Being vulnerable can help us avoid the trap of cool. If you want to know where to start, watch Brené Brown's TED talk on the power of vulnerability.[6] It's been viewed by millions of people. I think it's the fourth-most-watched TED talk of all time. It's well worth twenty minutes of your time.

I used to pretend to be cool, but I feel more like a nerdy loner at heart. I make corny jokes. When I speak, I'm not eloquent. Like the apostle Paul, I don't write or preach with wise and persuasive words. And that used to just drive me nuts. But not anymore. I'm learning to be okay with who I've been made to be. And being open and vulnerable about these things has been a big step in that direction.

So this week practice being yourself in your conversations. Not trying to impress or dominate, but being the real you. Just you. That's enough.

CHAPTER EIGHT

Open Your Eyes and Ears

Nonstarter: Keep the conversation superficial.
Opener: Discern what's really going on with people.

HAVE YOU EVER BEEN IN A CONVERSATION when all of a sudden you wonder what's going on? If that person really just said what you thought they said? Jesus never had that problem. He was amazing at seeing beneath the surface. I wish I could "know" the way Jesus seemed to know what was going on—really going on.

Jesus took nothing at face value. It's true that he had the unfair advantage of divinity, but because he was tempted in all things, as we are, I have to assume he also was tempted to miss what was really happening in the unseen world around him.

His conversations were direct or confusing or simple or complex, all depending on the person and the situation. He was incredibly intentional with how he used conversation, because he never wanted to stay on the surface of things. When the person needed one more question to get to a place of understanding, he asked one more question. When they needed a challenge to reframe their perspective, he challenged them.

Jesus was able to discern and truly see what was happening behind the scenes in each person's life. And we have that ability as well. We just have to learn to use it.

Try this one. In Matthew 16, we find a classic conversation between Jesus and the Pharisees and Sadducees. The religious leaders came to him to test him (actually, to trick him) and asked him to "show them a sign from heaven."[1]

Jesus replied, "When evening comes, you say, 'It will be fair weather, for the sky is red,' and in the morning, 'Today it will be stormy, for the sky is red and overcast.' You know how to interpret the appearance of the sky, but you cannot interpret the signs of the times."[2]

Eh?

What kind of conversationalist is this? If we're learning to have good conversations from Jesus, well, frankly, this one doesn't seem to give us much to work with. It leaves me a little puzzled. And maybe that's the point. The Pharisees and Sadducees were trying to trap Jesus, and he saw right through it. So he neatly sidestepped their trap and left them scratching their heads.

There are tons of such moments throughout the Gospels, where Jesus takes a question and totally turns it on its head. Remember the so-called rich young ruler of Mark's Gospel?[3]

He came to Jesus, fell at his feet, and contritely asked, "Good teacher, what must I do to inherit eternal life?"[4]

Now, if it were me, I probably would have jumped at the open door of this question from the rich young ruler to lay out the step-by-step plan for salvation. But not Jesus. He paid attention to the man, refusing to push past him with his own preplanned agenda.

Jesus first gave him a little rebuke, saying that no one is good except his Father in heaven. (Huh?) Then he proceeded to answer by giving the ruler a quick review of the Ten Commandments, which the man had supposedly been following.

But then *wham*—outta nowhere, Jesus blindsided the poor guy, asking him to sell all his stuff and give it to the poor.

Come on, man! That is totally unfair. Why would he do that? The poor guy went away sad, because he was wealthy. That would've made me sad too. But Jesus saw beneath the question to the man's heart and challenged him: Was his heart with his riches, or with Jesus and his Kingdom?

The rich man presented an honorable question. Jesus gave a slight rebuke.

Jesus tested his theology and practice. The honorable man passed the test.

But then came the tough question. The honorable man folded under the pressure.

And so the disciples were confused.

Of course, Jesus never failed to use such times as teaching moments for his disciples. As they watched the rich man go and wondered who could be saved if not him, Jesus responded to their amazement and confusion by saying that it's hard for people with lots of stuff to let go and enter into God's Kingdom. But then he told them the good news: Things we find impossible, God can make possible.

Because Jesus was constantly listening to his Father, he knew the heart of the rich young ruler and the hearts of his confused followers. And like Jesus, we also can listen to the Father and get better at discerning people's hearts.

Of course, it takes some practice. Lots of practice.

My natural eyes aren't that good—they went kaput when I turned fifty—and my spiritual eyes still need a lot of training. While I was working on this book, my wife and I spent some time at a friend's house in Mexico so I could focus on writing. One day we met a woman from China who was trying to sell us something, and we fairly successfully did all the things I talked about in the first section of this book. We were kind to her. We said hi. We acknowledged her as a human. We asked her questions. We did something small for her (we bought what she was selling us). Her kid wasn't there, but we found out his name and really got to know him through her.

And we were fully present with her. We saw her three days straight and each time took time to speak with her. We became friends.

The last time we were with her just talking, she started to really open up. My first reaction, being the godly author that I am, was to move on. I was busy writing a book about having great conversations with people like Jesus, and I didn't have time to be interrupted by one now.

But that thought was fleeting and I stayed put. (Chris

pinching me under the table probably helped.) As we talked, Chris and I both felt like we should ask if we could pray for her. Usually she is quickest to go there, but I found out later that she was thinking I should do it. So as the conversation wound down, I just said, "Can we pray for you? It seems you could use God to touch you."

The woman had already shared with us that she had no faith. I think "no religion" was the phrase she used. But we've always found that when people are in need, it doesn't matter what they think they have or don't have, what they believe or don't believe—they're happy for prayer!

We bowed our heads right there at the table, outside in the middle of everything—with her coworkers looking on— and prayed. Actually, she and Chris bowed their heads and closed their eyes. Me, still being a bit too cool for that, kept my eyes open and my head up. Didn't want people to think we were weird or something (sad, isn't it?).

Everything in me wants to write a powerful God encounter into these next lines. Or at least that she broke down and cried all over Chris's arm, making her sleeve wet. But no. Nothing, really. She said, "Wow, that was nice" and "Thank you guys *so* much." She was clearly touched by our love and concern. And we haven't seen her since.

So that's it. Not a very big hurdle. Chris and I paid attention to what was going on underneath the surface. We cared deeply about the woman in front of us. We both "heard from God" that we should pray, and we did. The results are up to God. And that's not just a spiritual-sounding thing to say, although it probably is good basic theology, but it's true. The results really are up to him. And we'll likely never know what happened after we left.

So this week walk around trying to listen to God in order to get beneath the surface of conversations. If you haven't done much of that, here's what I'd suggest to get going:

1. Pray something like "God, I need help hearing from you."
2. When you talk to people in any setting, try tuning in to the other channel that's happening at the same time the person is talking: the God channel. Then just see if something comes to mind as you're talking.
3. Act on whatever comes to mind. You can say, "Hey, I just had this pop into my head while we've been talking. Does that ring true?" (or "Does that have any relevance?").

Do this for years and you'll get really good at seeing what Jesus sees. When he told his disciples to open their eyes to see that the harvest was ripe,[5] I imagine he said that because he knew their eyes wouldn't otherwise be open. When our eyes are open, our conversations change.

CHAPTER NINE

Accept That You Are Not God

Nonstarter: Think too highly of yourself.
Opener: Be humble.

I HAD A GOOD FRIEND MANY YEARS AGO who was an ex-convict, struggled with alcoholism and drug abuse (I was his Narcotics Anonymous sponsor), and worked with me in construction. He loved to say (like, every time I saw him), "Carl, there's only one thing I know: There is a God and I ain't it." And then he'd laugh and sort of lean back as if he'd discovered something profound. And I think he had.

Jesus is God. I'm not.

Jesus *is* divine, yet in his time on earth, he was always, consistently, incredibly humble. Jesus exhibited humility throughout his life again and again.

Jesus said he could do only what the Father was doing. That there were certain things he didn't know. (Even Jesus wasn't a know-it-all. Think on that one a bit.)

He stayed silent in the face of untrue and unfair criticism. He never overstated his mission to make a point.

Jesus was humble.

Now, before we go further, let's define *humility*, because it gets a bad rap. *Webster's* does a pretty good job: "the quality or state of not thinking you are better than other people."[1] I like to put a spiritual twist on it by defining it simply as seeing ourselves as God sees us. Not more. Not less.

Jesus did that. He was comfortable in his own skin. He knew his place. He wasn't a wimp or a pushover. He was strong. Tough. Resolute. Committed. Outspoken. Controversial. He wasn't weak.

And he was surely the humblest person who ever lived. It's possible to be both strong and humble.

My story of journeying with humility is a mixed bag. On the positive side, I know myself pretty well and am willing to own it. I'm pretty good at being self-effacing, especially when I speak. I enjoy poking fun at myself and don't take myself too seriously.

I'm also fairly good at knowing what I'm not good at and what I am good at. I'm a very good public speaker. I hold an audience and communicate clearly. I know that. I'm a decent writer, but not great. I'm technically not good with how I string words and thoughts together, and my grammar and syntax are usually somewhere between poor and horrendous—and I use ellipses and dashes way too much to cover a run-on sentence . . . such as this one.

I know I'm a bad manager. Not a very good leader. But I'm really good at motivating people by jumping in head first and then encouraging others to do the same. Once we've all jumped in, I'm usually not great at knowing what to do next. I'm a great starter, an okay finisher, and really bad at the stuff in between.

So I'd say that's humility. I see myself for who I am. I don't often live in delusion or deception.

Nevertheless, I'm tempted to think more highly of myself than I should. And I'm insecure, which often leads to pride. I wonder too much about what other people are thinking about me and what I'm doing. I get embarrassed and defensive easily. I think about what you're thinking about what I'm thinking about what you're thinking. Humility doesn't do that. Humility is not thinking less of yourself but thinking of yourself less.

In my interactions with people, I have to be aware of who I am, both good and bad, my strengths and my weaknesses. Only then can I come to them openhanded, quicker to listen and slower to respond, free of the need to prove myself to myself, to God, or to anyone else. Which enables me to simply *be* in a conversation, without forcing an outcome.

The person I have the most conversations with is my wife, Chris. We talk every day. Even when I travel, we at least text and usually connect by phone every day. She's a lot humbler than I am, but she's also a strong-willed Greek lady. And as you might guess, that sometimes leads to conflict. (Shhhh, don't tell anyone.)

When I'm being humble in my conversations with her, I'm quicker to listen and slower to judge what I think she's saying. I slow down my response and wait for her to finish.

In fact, she'll often start off a topic she knows might strike a nerve with "Now, don't say anything until I'm done." She says that because I'm likely to break every rule I've just written about. The challenge in having great conversations in marriage—at least in ours—is not to assume too much. Chris and I know we're together for life, so we take a lot for granted when the other person is talking.

But, of course, that's ridiculous.

When there's humility in our conversations, they go oh-so-much better. Like 100 percent better. (Which I've been trying to tell Chris for years, but . . .)

So let's start with being humble in our closest relationships. With our family. Don't assume. Ask questions. Wait to say what you think and really listen first. When you are asked a question and don't know the answer, just say, "I don't know." Humble yourself. See what new arenas of conversation might open up. Practicing this intentionally with the people we're most likely to make assumptions with will help us be more present and purposeful in all our interactions.

This week let's work together on being humble in our conversations. Let's move in quiet confidence with what we do know and let go of all the things we aren't so sure of. Let's resist saying everything that comes to mind. When we do have something important to say, let's say it clearly and resist repeating ourselves. Let's be confident but not cocky, and above all, let's be good listeners, which is the highest form of humility in a conversation.

CHAPTER TEN

Don't Be So Strategic

Nonstarter: Overthink everything.
Opener: Just go with it sometimes.

IN SOME WAYS, JESUS WAS VERY STRATEGIC. He was clear about his goals, his purpose, his mission and vision, in a Jesus-y sort of way. But when we talk about leadership and strategy and all that good stuff, we don't typically look at Jesus. I haven't seen many books—even Christian books—written about any of those things from a Jesus-centered perspective. Authors tend to draw from others such as Moses, Nehemiah, Joshua, and the apostle Paul. All great examples, by the way, but they're not Jesus.

And I think I know why we don't generally associate Jesus with strategy. His strategy was pretty *non*strategic. It's hard to come up with a three-point list to describe how he worked. I've tried to analyze his life and look for common threads of strategy, and, well, it's almost impossible. He allowed himself to be interrupted constantly by seemingly nonstrategic people. Whenever things really started moving forward, he either said something that would surely stop the momentum or just up and left.

One of my all-time favorite nonstrategic Jesus moments is in John 6, at the end of his beautiful discourse on the bread of life. He concluded his sermon by dropping this little bread bomb: "Unless you eat the flesh of the Son of Man and drink his blood, you have no life in you."[1]

There you go. Eat his flesh and drink his blood. Imagine sitting on your favorite bench in that synagogue, hearing him tell you that while he's standing right there in front of you. Yuck.

John goes on to note that many of the disciples found this to be a "hard teaching."[2] You think?

Jesus then asked, "Does this offend you?"[3]

Um . . . yes, it offended many, as "many of his disciples turned back and no longer followed him."[4]

Now, if I were Jesus, everything in my church-growth paradigm and strategic ministry handbook would encourage me to grab the disciples as they're about to leave and explain what I meant. Obviously, Jesus couldn't have literally meant to eat his physical body and drink his actual blood—that would be cannibalism. At the very least, he should have explained himself to the ones who stayed.

But he did neither. He just asked those who stuck with him if they wanted to leave as well.

Not very strategic, I'd say. At least not in how we measure strategy.

I mentioned earlier in this book that Jesus didn't mind offending people. The rich young ruler. The crowd in the synagogue at Nazareth when he used a Lebanese woman and a Syrian official as the examples of God's grace being poured out in the fulfillment of Isaiah 61. Jesus offended people over and over again. The very ones who could have helped spread his message—those in positions of leadership, such as Roman and Jewish politicians and religious authorities—he offended.

The ones he was kindest and gentlest with were those on the outskirts of society. Lepers. Beggars. Samaritans. Women and children. Even the twelve young men he initially called to make his closest followers weren't people of position or power. It was often noted in the most derogatory of ways that these men were "from Galilee,"[5] which was a poor, nondescript part of Israel. They were small businessmen, at most. Young. Untrained. Fishermen—a generally rough, unkempt lot. We really know much about only three of Jesus' disciples: Peter, James and John. The others didn't make much of a splash, or, in the case of Judas, they made the wrong kind of impression.

Again, doesn't seem like much of a strategy.

Maybe the problem is my idea of "strategic." Even though I've lived much of my adult life outside the US, I still have a very Western mind-set about what my strategy should be. I should be able to write it down, articulate it in an elevator speech, defend it both privately and publicly, and above all know it and live it deeply and consistently. And all of those things are good things, by the way. Nothing wrong with any of them. They're just not what Jesus did with his life.

The reason I think this is so important for our understanding of Jesus' conversation styles—and ultimately ours—is because when we place undue importance on strategy, our conversations become unnatural and even downright weird. Believe me, I know.

When I was twenty-one, I went through a program at our church called Evangelism Explosion (EE). I was pretty good at what it entailed, so I became a trainer. It's a wonderful program designed to help churches follow up with visitors and create an opportunity to lead people to Christ. People new to the church fill out a form indicating they are open to a visit from someone from the church, and then an EE trainer contacts the person and schedules a time.

I went on many such visits. People were generally thankful that I and the other trainers came, and we tried our very best to be kind, gracious presenters of the Good News. It was strategy at its best.

We basically plunged right in with "the two questions." The first question was something like "If you were to die tonight, do you know if you'd go to heaven?" A little intense, but it definitely got things moving.

The second question was similar: "If you stood at the gates of heaven and God said to you, 'Why should I let you into my heaven?' what would you say?"

Not much subtlety there, for sure. Would I ever do anything like this again? No way.

The challenge is this: We can have tons of conversations with people who don't know Jesus. We can use the Roman Road (Romans 3, 5, 6, and 10), the Bridge diagram, the EE strategy, and the Four Spiritual Laws—and be clear, concise, and even effective. Strategic in the best sense of its Western definition.

But a strategy doesn't lead to real conversation. By definition, conversation is two people (or more) having a real-time, give-and-take dialogue about something. The above-mentioned tools, which I used most of my early adult life, were simply monologues pretending to be conversations. It's as close to preaching as you can get without the pulpit.

But Jesus was a master at actual conversation. Each discussion went a different direction. He had no prearranged method of talking to people. No cookie-cutter mold.

I've had to learn how to have real, honest, back-and-forth conversations with people. It's been surprisingly difficult for someone who is supposedly in the people business. It means laying down any agenda or strategy and letting the interaction happen on its own terms. Real conversations involve really listening, to the person and to the Holy Spirit. As we've talked about before, it means asking questions based on what you've heard. And in a good conversation, don't be thinking ahead to how you have the answer to the person's particular issue, or a good story to follow theirs. Resist the temptation to know what to say next. Let the other person take the lead.

If you do these things, most of the time you'll have a great conversation—one in which the person feels truly cared about and heard because they feel like a priority, not a project. And walls come down when people feel cared about and heard.

Our neighbors invited us over a few nights ago for drinks and to catch up on our most recent trip to Dubai. They are good-hearted, universalist, live-and-let-live sorts of folks. The kind you'd want for a neighbor. They started right off by saying how nice it is that everyone in Dubai lives together in peace and harmony (which is actually mostly true, at least on the surface) and that if the whole world would just be nice and tolerate each other's religions and preferences, we'd all get along.

There's a big part of me that agrees with that. Actually, it makes for a great plan for a great world. But I just don't agree with the premise that usually lies behind those thoughts.

In my years past, I would have probably jumped in and started down my preordained path of "That's not so because . . ." It's a good strategy, right? Correcting false assumptions in order to better pave the path for truth?

But I didn't do it. Because something that sounds like a good strategy can also shut a conversation down really quickly. So I just listened and mostly nodded my head and made small grunting noises. The kind where it really isn't clear if it's an agreement or not. The conversation continued along the syrupy edge of world peace and group hugs for quite some time without my saying a word otherwise. Anyway, who doesn't like syrup, world peace, and group hugs?

And it's good I didn't say much, because it soon came out that there had been some recent family drama in their lives—as in that very day. It was actually some pretty hard, weird stuff for them to deal with. The last thing they needed was a fundie like me yelling at them about how the world's a mess because it's rejected its Savior.

They said they wanted world peace, but really they were looking for inner peace. Tossing out the strategy allowed me to get to what was really on their hearts.

So my new strategy, aligned a bit more with Jesus, is to exhibit patient listening in real-life conversations that go wherever the person and God want them to go.

A life of patience and listening. Sounds a bit like love, which is the first and primary fruit of the Spirit.

Maybe this week we can try practicing patient listening with our friends, family, coworkers, and neighbors. Just "wasting time" with them, coming in with no preset purpose, no agenda. Drop the strategy. Allow them to lead the conversations. Then just be ready to jump in when it seems right. But if not, just grab a drink and enjoy the conversation for what it is.

The Final Word:
"Be Present"

BEING FULLY PRESENT for and to the people around us may be the key to everything in this book, and maybe to life itself. Jesus himself taught us to pray, "Give us *this* day our daily bread" (emphasis added).[1] Today's bread, not tomorrow's. Jesus wants to be with us, provide for us, lead us—now, in this moment that we have. And he wants us to be there for others, present with them, and with him, in the now. I've not always been great at this, but I'm getting better, and it's changing the way I do ministry, life, business, everything.

I think I can summarize much of what I've said in this section with one word: *relax*.

When my kids were teenagers, still living in our house, we'd make it a point to periodically go into their rooms at bedtime and lie down next to them for a chat. No agenda. I think back on those times fondly. Some of our best and deepest conversations happened during those bedtime chats. Defenses were down and we were relaxed. Nothing was waiting for us but sleep. And in that space, we could truly share and hear from one another.

Granted, we can have those bedtime chats only with

family. But my point is, just as my kids relaxed during those no-agenda conversations, people in general are more open to talking when they believe they're not a project. People can sense when we're uptight. They figure out pretty quickly when we have an agenda for them. Of course, we'd never say it's an agenda, because that sounds so negative. We'd just say we're living life on mission. Or have a purpose. Or maybe we'll use the *S* word: *strategy*. Whatever we call it, people are more perceptive than we give them credit for.

And if there's anything that will kill a healthy, lively conversation, it's a preconceived agenda.

It's time to reconsider the ways of Jesus. Put down your strategy. Choose authenticity. Be engaged with what's really happening. Enjoy each person you meet. And show the person in front of you that they mean more to you than your plans. You never know what might happen next.

DIG DEEPER & DISCUSS

1. Think of a person in your life who best demonstrates this quality of "presence." How do they make you feel? Is there anything specific that this person does that communicates value to you and makes you feel safe?

2. Read some of the Scripture passages referenced in this section (Genesis 16:7-14; Luke 4:18-27; 10:38-42). What story or conversation of Jesus best illustrates the quality of presence to you?

3. This week we were challenged to be present with the people around us. Which of the following did you attempt? How did it go?

   a. Focus on being present in the conversations you have. Stop multitasking. Listen.

   b. Be yourself in conversations. Stop trying to impress or dominate.

   c. Listen to God while you talk to people. Invite him into your interactions.

   d. Practice humility in your conversations, especially with those in your family and others closest to you.

   e. Let go of your agenda and strategy and just go with it.

3 Be Brave

I learned that courage was not the absence of fear, but the triumph over it. The brave man is not he who does not feel afraid, but he who conquers that fear. NELSON MANDELA

The high priest asked him, "Are you the Messiah, the Son of the Blessed One?"

"I am," said Jesus. "And you will see the Son of Man sitting at the right hand of the Mighty One and coming on the clouds of heaven." MARK 14:61-62

Jesus was a brave man. I would argue, the bravest. Full of courage unlike anyone in history. It took courage to give up heaven and come to earth. Courage to be born a little baby, helpless and vulnerable. Courage to live the kind of life he lived, confronting the powers of religious authoritarianism and raw Roman power. Courage to choose to die—and go through with it. Then, after all that work, living and dying among us, courage to leave.

Coming. Staying. Leaving. It all took tremendous courage.

Jesus conversed with boldness and courage. He knew that his words and actions would cost him his life, but he didn't shrink back.

So if Jesus is our model, we must follow him with bravery and courage in our day-to-day interactions. Take risks. Mess up. Say the wrong thing but then have the courage to go back and try for a redo.

Otherwise, we'll languish in the backwaters of boredom, doing nothing but rehashing weather and sports. Don't get me wrong—I love a good tornado show on the Weather Channel, and sports is probably my favorite pastime to both watch and play. But I don't want to be stuck in a place where that's all I can discuss with any sort of security and confidence.

If we're going to follow Jesus, we need to learn to walk on the wild side of topics. Go where we haven't gone before. It requires faith to step into the unknown, into risky conversations that can (and sometimes do) go bad. Conversations that cause your heart to explode when you're in the middle of them. When you're left emotionally, mentally, and spiritually exhausted after they're over.

Sound fun? You might be thinking, *No, it doesn't. It sounds horrible.* And you might be right. Faith is spelled *r-i-s-k*. And the thing with risk is that it's risky. You could get hurt. You probably will get hurt at times. Lose some sleep. Set a friendship back after many years of work. Make someone mad at you for a long time, or worse, lose that person altogether. It's possible.

But I'll tell you this: Without being brave in your conversations and willing to risk rejection or suffering of some kind, you won't have much reward.

Before we go further and dig into what it really means to be brave in our conversations, I have to clarify something. Pointing out the hard sayings of Jesus is not usually my thing. People such as the Westboro Baptists, the Ku Klux Klan, the Crusaders of the Middle Ages, and so many other groups have twisted the words of Jesus and Scripture to justify some really, really horrible stuff. These words have been terribly misused over the centuries, and I'm so sorry for that.

Jesus does not model tearing people apart whenever we feel like it. But he does model how to be bold in our speech, with love. So to follow Jesus' example and avoid falling into the trap of misusing God's Word, let's note three very important methods for understanding Scripture:

1. We interpret what might be confusing in light of what's clear.
2. We interpret the minority of verses through the lens of the majority.
3. We recognize context.

In light of these three methods, I think it's safe to say this:

1. Jesus' message was one of light, love, peace, joy, and invitation. He wanted and still wants everyone to believe in and follow him.
2. The vast majority of the Gospels involves Jesus healing the hurting and setting people free, not keeping people out.

3. The context of Jesus' hard sayings is almost exclusively aimed at those in power, those who abused their power, and those who distorted or stood against this new Kingdom that Jesus proclaimed.

It's therefore quite safe to say that Jesus' hard words were for a very specific few in a very specific context. We should never assume we can use such language at will just because Jesus did. Instead, we should look at the heart behind the words. The motives behind the bravery. It was always about the person. About what was going to wake them up, point them to God, draw them into the wild and beautiful Kingdom. Bravery isn't bravery if your ego and need to be right get in the way. True bravery is bold love. True bravery is being like Jesus.

CHAPTER ELEVEN

Find Your Barley Field

Nonstarter: Fight about everything.
Opener: Know when to take a stand.

JESUS EXHIBITED TREMENDOUS BRAVERY throughout his life. That's why we always want to lean on and look to Jesus' words and actions first. But when we're talking about being brave, we can be tempted to say we're too small or not strong enough or not smart enough. No matter how much we acknowledge Jesus' humanity, we still might dismiss his bravery as out of our league. Which is why I'd first like to look at another normal person like you and me.

We meet this guy in a small and slightly obscure story that's been one of my favorites since I was a child. He was one of King David's so-called "three mighty men." He wasn't the chief of the three, just one of the three. His name was Eleazar, son of Dodai the Ahohite.

Here's his story:

Next to [David] was Eleazar son of Dodai the
Ahohite, one of the three mighty warriors. He was
with David at Pas Dammim when the Philistines
gathered there for battle. At a place where there
was a field full of barley, the troops fled from the
Philistines. But they took their stand in the middle
of the field. They defended it and struck the
Philistines down, and the LORD brought about
a great victory.[1]

Here's the general idea: David and his army of Israelites,
with his mighty men at his side, were fighting but getting
walloped by the Philistines. The whole army retreated except
for Eleazar. Or except for him and David, as the writer of
Chronicles records it. Either way, Eleazar alone, or Eleazar
with King David, dug his feet into the barley field, stood
his ground, and single-handedly turned the tide against the
Philistines.

For the sake of a good metaphor, I want to point something out. Ancient Israel was a very fruitful place. Corn,
wheat, avocados, grapes, and oranges all grew plentifully in
the region. But we hear nothing about Eleazar taking a stand
in the vineyard, the orchard, or even the cornfield. Nope. He
took his stand among the barley spikes.

Eleazar's story teaches us something very important about
being brave. Bravery doesn't mean fighting every single
battle. It means having the wisdom to find our barley fields:
the places of our uncompromising stands.

Jesus had a few barley fields. But before we go there,

let's acknowledge that there were several "fields" that others thought he *should* take a stand in.

The woman caught in adultery should have been stoned, according to the law.[2] Jesus' affirmation should have been a no-brainer, according to the Pharisees. But not to Jesus. Their judgment was not a field in which he would take a stand.

Jesus' followers were picking grain on the Sabbath, breaking the law.[3] This was clear cause for harsh rebuke according to the religious crowd. But not according to Jesus.

Lazy Mary needed a swift kick in the proverbial bum, according to Martha.[4] But not according to Jesus.

Jesus didn't take the bait in any of these situations. He refused to take the conversational stand that others expected of him. (Which was, in itself, taking a different kind of stand.) But then we get to Peter.

Things seemed to be going pretty well relationally for Peter and Jesus. Peter had proven his faith by walking on the water and had even been blessed by Jesus for the brilliant spiritual insight, revealed by God himself, that Jesus was the Messiah. In fact, as a result, Jesus planned to give Peter the keys to the Kingdom. Peter must have been feeling pretty good. So good, in fact, that he felt confident to rebuke Jesus and tell him that "never" would Jesus' prediction of his suffering and death occur. Bad move.

"Get behind me, Satan!" Jesus exclaimed. "You are a hindrance to me. For you are not setting your mind on the things of God, but on the things of man."[5]

Whoa. Peter had crossed a line, stepped smack-dab into

Jesus' barley field, and was called the worst name in the book. By Jesus. Bad day.

So, as we see from Eleazar and Jesus, being brave in our conversations doesn't mean we take on every issue. For instance, I'm 100 percent pro-life. I'm against abortion for any reason. I'm also antiwar and anti–capital punishment. I like to say that I'm pro-life from womb to tomb. Catchy, eh?

But of those three life issues, I speak out on only one. I doubt you've ever heard me say or seen me write anything about abortion or capital punishment. But I say a lot about war. While our family lived in the Middle East, our lives were directly affected by war, so that one feels more personal and I feel uniquely compelled to speak out about it.

Another one of my barley fields related to war is Jesus' love for Muslims. No matter how hard you push, you cannot convince me that Jesus is against Muslims or that Muslims are inherently bad people. It is my experience that Muslims, as much as any people, can respond quite readily and positively when presented with the Good News that Jesus most clearly shows them their true Father.

Recently, I took a trip into Somalia. Yes, you read that right: Somalia. Dear Somalian Muslim friends of ours invited us to go. Somalia is plagued by drought, famine, and the threatening presence of Al-Shabaab. It's not a place a lot of people want to visit.

As some of our Western and Middle Eastern friends began to hear of my decision, the pushback came: "It's too dangerous!"; "You can't trust them!"; "It's irresponsible!"; "You won't make a difference." But unbeknownst to them,

I was standing in my barley field, committed to following Jesus into a situation I thought he wanted me in, in a war zone among my Muslim friends. Some direct words were exchanged between us, and I realized that some of them will never understand or agree. But I took my conversational, and physical, stand and went to Somalia.

While I admit that going into Somalia makes me sound pretty brave, actually I chicken out fairly regularly. Countless times, I've been presented with a clear opportunity for a great conversation and I give it a pass. Sometimes because I'm just too tired. Maybe I'm sick. Or both sick and tired—of people. That happens.

Maybe I don't jump in because I'm tired of controversy and just can't take any more right at that moment. There are all sorts of reasons. But when that happens, I get back up, remind myself of where I feel God has asked me to take a stand and where he hasn't, and ask him for fresh courage.

This week spend some time thinking about what you're most passionate about in conversations and why. Do you try to be knowledgeable and ready for a fight in too many arenas? For what are you willing to speak up and bear the consequences of doing so? And when have you done that when it was unnecessary or inappropriate? Be honest with yourself.

CHAPTER TWELVE

Stand Alone (When Necessary)

Nonstarter: Always go with the crowd.
Opener: Humbly go it alone.

JESUS WAS OFTEN ALONE. Yes, he had a team and some very close friends he spent tons of time with, but you'll often find him alone in the Gospels.

This is a highly nuanced point about the life of Jesus. Mostly I would encourage you, and me, to live in community. Like, all the time. Be with good people whom you can learn and grow and serve with. You know the old adage "If you want to go fast, go alone. If you want to go far, go together." And it's true.

Jesus chose twelve men to walk with. He also seemed to choose about the same number of women to always be around and be part of the great Team Jesus, making about twenty-five men and women in total. These people were with him, and he was with them. They were fully committed to one another.

He also spent more time with three of them, who were his little band of brothers: Peter, James, and John. And among them—at least according to John—he had a best friend. Yes, you guessed it: John.

The Gospel writers referenced larger circles of Jesus followers as well. There were the crowds, thousands of them, interested enough in Jesus (and his miracles) to risk running out of food to follow him across the lake. And there were the 120, gathered in community after his crucifixion. We see the seventy-two who were very committed, sent out by Jesus to neighboring villages to show what Jesus' Kingdom was like.

So Jesus had the crowds, the 120, the seventy-two, the twenty-five, the twelve, the three, and the one. Like most of us.

If you're relatively normal in how you do relationships, you'll have loads of acquaintances and a hundred or so "friends"—people you know by first and last name and see somewhat regularly.

And then you might have about twenty-five or so who you would call for help of some kind.

And twelve whom you'd count as real friends. Three who are really close friends. And one best friend.

Jesus was actually pretty normal in his friendship circles. Imagine that. He really did live not just among us but like us. And he recognized his need for friends. Community. People to share his ups and downs with. Do you think he was just faking discouragement when he came back and found his three BFFs sound asleep on the most dramatically horrible night of his life? No way. He was totally and completely bummed. And he let them know!

Jesus had real friends, real enemies, and real conversations. Some of the conversations went well, and some . . . not so much. But he lived out his life in the midst of community.

Nonetheless, sometimes he stood alone. All by himself. He said things that alienated others and made decisions that no one else understood or agreed with.

Do you remember early in Jesus' ministry when he and his new disciples were in Capernaum? He had just endeared himself to Peter by healing the fisherman's mother-in-law.[1] The sick and demon possessed were being set free.[2] The book of Mark says that "the whole town gathered at the door."[3] By all accounts, it was a great night.

But early the next morning, Jesus sneaked out to get some time alone to pray. Reading into his motives a bit, I think he understood the temptation to go with the crowd. To continue today what was right for yesterday. So he pulled away for perspective. To have a conversation with his dad.

His solitude was cut short by the intrusion of Peter and his friends exclaiming, essentially, "What the heck are you doing? Everyone is looking for you! You should get back and keep doing miracles like yesterday!"[4]

But Jesus made a different decision. That time alone gave him discernment and courage to stand alone, even from his closest friends. To risk being misunderstood in order to choose what he believed to be right and best. So they got up and left.

Jesus had many *Braveheart* moments. And there were others in the Bible who had courage to go it alone when necessary. Mary. Paul. Peter. David. Rahab. Joshua. Those who chose the lonely path were many.

So here's the tricky part: How do you know when to go with your conviction that no one agrees with, or when to listen to your team of friends and be willing to leave your conviction at the altar?

It's tough. I haven't been right on this one all that often. I've yielded to outside pressure when I should have stood my ground alone. And I've stubbornly dug in my heels when I should have listened to others.

Here's what I've learned so far—a general rule of thumb that may help. The great majority of the time, it's wise to listen to and heed the advice of your spouse, family, and close trusted friends. Those who have committed themselves to walking with you, to standing behind you no matter what. Those with track records of giving you wise counsel. Then on the rare occasion when you just know that you have to stand up and say something to someone or do something that isn't popular, do it. If it turns out you're wrong, admit it and move on.

Back to my Somalia trip. 'Twas the night before we were to fly in. My companions and I were relaxing before our big trip, when we heard the news that the head of the region we needed to fly through had threatened to shoot us down upon entering his airspace. At first we thought he was bluffing, but with some legitimate investigation, we learned that not only was he serious but he had the capacity to follow through with his threats. We talked. We prayed. We wrung our hands. We had counted the cost of traveling to Somalia, but we hadn't factored this one into the equation. At the end of the night, my friends, including the pilot, decided it was too risky. I don't relish death threats. Although I really do look forward to meeting Jesus face-to-face, I like my life. I'm not quite ready to leave it yet.

But I knew I needed to go. I'd felt God speak to me in an unusually clear way about going to Somalia. So I let them know that, if need be, I'd go in alone.

Long story short, we all went in. And we didn't get shot down. And it turned out that the threat by this neighboring leader was instrumental to our getting to actually meet him and introduce ourselves and get his blessing to help the people of Somalia. So, thankfully, it all turned out okay. But it might not have. That was the risk I was taking in standing alone.

When you think you need to make a risky decision or confront someone or say something difficult you think they need to hear, run it by your spouse or a couple of people who know you well. Listen carefully to what they have to say. But in the end, it's your choice to make.

This week think of how you might step out and be brave and perhaps go against the grain. It might be inviting a neighbor to dinner, having a conversation with one of your kids about something that isn't quite right, or talking to a coworker who needs to know that you care enough to share your faith. Take a conversational risk. Step out. You might feel alone, and you might actually *be* alone. And that's okay, because you do have one who is with you! If it doesn't work out the way you feel it should, humble yourself. Trust God to accomplish what he wants in spite of your mistakes and imperfections.

CHAPTER THIRTEEN

Say Something Crazy

Nonstarter: Carefully manage your reputation.
Opener: Risk looking foolish.

JESUS DIDN'T SEEM TO MIND looking foolish. What do you think his neighbors, family members, and friends thought of him when he said and did certain things? I'm sure there were plenty of raised eyebrows, sidelong glances, and whispers behind his back. After all, he told his closest followers that they needed to eat his flesh and drink his blood. Not surprisingly, they freaked out.

And then there was that time he put mud on the blind man's eyes.[1] He'd healed blind people before, without mud. "Come on, Jesus. Is that really necessary? A bit dramatic, isn't it?" Or that time he told the Jews to destroy this temple and he'd raise it again in three days. What? The temple they were thinking of took forty-six years to build.[2] It's true that later on, they understood. But Jesus didn't seem to mind the lapse in reputational esteem.

When he drove out the religious crooks in the temple, I'm fairly sure no one saw it as a wise and heroic event. Religious leaders were generally held in high honor by the people in the community. The people probably looked at each other, rolled their eyes, and said, "Surely he's lost it."

Again and again, Jesus was willing to look foolish for the sake of a higher calling and purpose that only he fully understood. Bottom line, he cared more about obeying his Father and loving the people in front of him than how he was perceived.

Jesus wasn't the only one in the long line of biblical "heroes of faith" who were willing to look foolish for a bigger purpose yet to be revealed. Moses told Pharaoh, "Let my people go."[3] Ruth stayed with Naomi, saying, "Your people will be my people and your God my God."[4] Hosea asked the prostitute Gomer to marry him.[5]

I could go on and on with the biblical examples, but let me just say that I take great confidence from this list of those who have "foolishly" gone on before you and me, and I readily follow their lead.

That trip to Somalia, for example. *Devastating* doesn't quite describe what we saw in Somalia. People, livestock, crops—so much death and dying due to war, poverty, and drought. At the time of our visit, it had been thirteen months since they'd seen a drop of rain. A question emanated from my heart: *God, is there anything we can do to help? Anything?*

Well, apparently, my friend Ali had an idea. Surrounded

one afternoon by a thousand or so locals coming to the well in search of water, he proudly announced, "Sheikh Carl will now pray for rain."

I looked toward Ali with what could rightly be called a glare. What was he thinking?

Now, I love a powerful-prayer-miracle story like anyone else, but this was not how I imagined it happening. I was emotional, trying to reconcile the devastation in front of me with my understanding of a loving and powerful God. I felt no surge of faith or surety that I "knew" that God would answer. I was hot. And tired. And, honestly, a bit angry that Ali had put me on the spot.

And so I stood, with two thousand eyes on me, feeling somewhat faithless. But Ali had faith. Faith to risk his reputation as a regional leader by inviting this white American Jesus follower to pray for a miracle. What could I do?

Thankfully, in that moment, I was motivated by something greater than fear of how I would look if I prayed and nothing happened. The people in front of me were suffering. And they had invited me to come before God on their behalf and ask for rain. So what was there for me to lose . . . that really mattered? Nothing.

So I decided to look foolish. I prayed for rain in the name of Jesus. Ali translated. It wasn't dramatic and I didn't feel inspired, but I was sincere. And when I finished, Ali leaned over to me and said, "Don't worry, Carl. I believe."

The next day, it rained. After thirteen months of drought. And those who knew of my prayer saw it as an act of God. Pretty cool, huh?

Of course, things don't always work out like that. You wouldn't be at risk of looking foolish if you didn't sometimes end up looking like a fool.

A few weeks after the rain in Somalia, I was sitting with two businessmen, talking life, politics, business, and well—you know—Jesus. I smoothly brought him into the conversation (as I do) by saying something super clever like "You know, that reminds me of something Jesus once said." And *bam*—the conversation was over. It just went dead cold. It felt as though a bucket of ice had been dumped on our heads and spilled onto the table where we were having lunch. The conversation got awkward and never recovered.

So there you go. This stuff isn't magic. We don't wave a wand and say some abracadabra spell and *shazam*, we're having an amazing Jesus conversation, and God makes it rain, and someone is healed, and wars turn to peace. In fact, many times this "looking foolish" thing just doesn't work at all. Jesus always works, but sometimes I don't.

And that's okay. We get up and carry on.

Let's be honest. We sometimes don't talk to people, or bring up Jesus, or have deep conversations, or pray when we should because we're afraid of looking foolish or feeling awkward. After all, people might not appreciate our asking where they worship, if they have a faith of some kind, if they believe in God, or whether their mom, who you prayed for last week, actually got better (because what if she didn't?). Right?

Here's the thing: Being foolish for Jesus in our everyday interactions can have profound impact on how those interactions go. We all have a myriad of choices to make in any conversation. What if we choose to turn the what-ifs around? What if instead of looking foolish, you get to watch the person in front of you have a powerful encounter with God? What if the person in front of you had a dream about Jesus last night and your "happening" to bring him up in conversation propels him to pursue God? What if your new acquaintance is longing for someone to invite her into something deeper and more meaningful than what she yet knows? What if we look foolish? Ah, come on. Who cares! What if we get to be conduits of the love of God in someone's life? It's a risk worth taking, if you ask me.

So this week let's all commit to risking looking like fools. To caring more about others than about how we're perceived. To asking questions in an attempt to go deeper. To talk about Jesus. Let's ask Jesus to set us free to be the best versions of ourselves for the sake of others, even if it means being fools for his sake.

CHAPTER FOURTEEN

Be Full of Grace (and Truth)

Nonstarter: Avoid conflict at all costs.
Opener: Speak a tough but necessary word to a friend.

SEVERAL TIMES IN THE GOSPELS, Jesus walked away from tough or awkward situations, and many times he avoided conflict. He would say something like "It isn't my time yet"[1] and walk on down the road. But there are plenty more occasions when he plunged right into the middle of hard conversations.

One such (extreme) example is the story of the adulterous woman we mentioned a few chapters back. The religious leaders had just caught her in adultery, for which the punishment was death by stoning. They expected Jesus to take a stand in their field, but Jesus refused. Rather, he appeared on the scene and came up with a crowd stopper: "Let him who is without sin cast the first stone."[2] After the crowd dispersed,

Jesus turned to the guilty woman and asked, "Where are your accusers?" She said, "They're gone." And then Jesus made an outrageous statement: "And neither do I accuse you. Go and sin no more."[3] He set her free with both a pronouncement of grace and a warning to stop the destructive behavior. The Accuser of our souls is Satan, not Jesus. The Lord's "Go and sin no more" brings freedom. The woman was free. Literally. Emotionally. Spiritually.

But the Pharisees didn't let it go at that. (Hard-line religious people always seem to have to push the envelope.) As soon as the woman left, they were right back in the who's-right-who's-wrong fight with Jesus. They kept up quite the banter, and he said some really hard things to them.

When the Pharisees asked, "Where is your father?" Jesus replied with, "You do not know me or my father and where I go you cannot come because you will be dead in your sins."[4] Ouch. Not nice at all.

The Pharisees also played the "father Abraham" card. It was the pride of every Jew, a physical and spiritual birthright, that their father was Abraham.

But Jesus didn't even give them that. He made a statement that surely sent them over the edge: "If Abraham truly was your father, you would do what he did. But you're not—you're trying to kill me."[5]

Being told they weren't really sons of Abraham? Having their secret motive to kill Jesus exposed? That got 'em. They exclaimed, "We are *not* illegitimate children. God is our only Father."[6]

Here we go. Jesus must have had enough: "Why is my

language not clear to you? Because you are unable to hear what I say. You belong to your father, the devil, and you want to carry out your father's desires."[7]

All right, then.

The Pharisees were like angry ten-year-olds in their answer, saying something like "You are too and more of it." Okay, their actual words were, "Aren't we right in saying that you are a Samaritan and demon-possessed?"[8] Junior high all over again.

It went back and forth like that a few more times until finally Jesus brought down the house: "I tell you the truth, before Abraham was ever born, I AM!"[9] And the Jews picked up stones and tried to kill him. Most likely because they were sick of the discussion, which wasn't moving in their favor, and partly because it seemed he had just claimed divinity with that "I AM" thing. After all, "I AM" is the name God gave himself in the Old Testament.

When was the last time you talked to someone like that? By the way, I am not encouraging you to go around telling religious leaders that they belong to the devil. It won't go well and it's not what Jesus instructed us to do. I'm pretty sure we're always to err on the side of love. The great commandments say just that.[10] I'm simply using this as an example of a tough conversation. It's tempting for me to think of Jesus as solely full of grace, but actually he was full of both grace and truth.

Chris and I often have discussions about certain situations with people and how much we should lean on the side of grace or on the side of truth. She tends to be more the truth teller. I'm more the grace giver. Neither by itself is like Jesus, who is full of both grace *and* truth.

He offered nearly unthinkable grace to the woman caught in adultery, and then he brought out the sledgehammer of truth when the Pharisees interrogated him. Let the irony sink in before we move on: to the clearly sinful woman, grace abounds; to the respected leaders of his own blood and tradition, truth told in force.

During the time we spend each year in Dubai, Chris and I have taken up golfing. And by "taken up," I mean we're trying. We're really bad. So we've hired a coach (I think *golf pro* is the correct term): Jack from Australia. Jack is really good. He hits his nine iron one handed better than I hit my driver.

As Jack started to help Chris and me, we talked. Jack couldn't figure out exactly what I do, but he knew it had something to do with following Jesus. Jack said something like "I'm an atheist. Okay, well, maybe not an atheist, but I sure don't believe in a God who can let children die in Africa and let storms wipe out whole villages."

Chris and I took ten one-hour lessons from Jack and also spent additional time with him each week at the driving range. And when you spend this kind of time together, your conversations deepen. In fact, we started spending more time talking about Jesus and the stories of our lives than we did talking about golf. Jack was intrigued. "Open" might be a bit much, but he was definitely interested—lots of questions and not too much defensiveness. And if I can say so with any humility at all, I'm pretty good at the ol' Jesus conversation. It's sorta what I do. But after about twenty hours together, he hadn't really budged. We liked our time together a lot and were becoming good friends, but he just wasn't getting the "Jesus is awesome and is real and loves you" bit.

During our last week in Dubai before we came back to Colorado for the summer, we went golfing. It just so happened that our daughter Anna was over from Lebanon, and she came with us to play nine holes with Jack. As we golfed, Anna suggested to Jack, "Hey, you should take your wife and go visit my mom and dad's church one weekend."

Now, let me just say this before I continue: Inviting someone like Jack to church isn't usually my first play. That would normally come a little later, after we've met a few times, probably opened the Bible, and had some good, deep, open spiritual conversations. I don't typically recommend opening with "You should come to church" with a guy who can't believe in "a God who sends people to hell" and "lets babies die of AIDS."

But there we have it: Anna made the suggestion. It was out there. And boy oh boy, did he ever react. If I remember his exact words, I think they were—while he looked at me as if I had asked the question rather than our daughter—"Carl, there's as much chance of you jumping out of an airplane without a parachute as there is for me to walk through the doors of a church."

So . . . that's fairly clear.

And something just snapped in me. I won't even blame it on God, as if he made me say this, but my response was— and I do remember my exact words—"Jack, do you know what your problem is?"

"Huh?" He looked frightened as he saw the look on my face.

"You've got no guts. You're afraid—of what, by the way? Are you afraid the God who doesn't exist is going to get you if you go to church? Or have you just been castrated? Come on, dude. Be a man. You can't come to church? What's the worst that will happen? It'll take an hour and a half out of your week—that's it. I'll be there to hold your hand if you get scared. But oh well. I doubt you'll do it. Whatever."

Those were pretty much my exact words. I've never said anything like that to anyone before and probably never will again.

He was in shock. He looked at me, mouth open and eyes the size of saucers. After an awkward five-second pause, he just said, "Okay, okay. I'll come. Gee whiz. Take it easy, man. I'll come. I'm not afraid. I'll come."

And that was that. He came to church with his wife and kids. And this story is unfolding as I write. That's where we are right now, real time. I yelled at the guy and he came to church. So what does that tell you? Actually, maybe not much. It's not a new form of evangelism. Don't take this too far, pretty please. Don't tell your pastor that this Medearis guy thinks you should bully people to get them to come to church. None of that. It's just a story to make a point:

Sometimes you need to have hard conversations.

Keeping it real, I must confess that I often chicken out when I know I should be tough. I blame it on grace. Being kind. I want to invite people, not offend them. I have spent a good portion of my life trying to help people see Jesus even though they thought they didn't want to see him. Mostly, I need to be nice to people and not turn into the preacher who yells with a bullhorn. But sometimes—I dunno, maybe 5 percent of the time—it's right to be tough or downright hard nosed. It sometimes comes across as mean (I'm guessing the Pharisees thought Jesus was mean) and the person often doesn't respond well, but you need to do it anyway.

Here are my three tips on when you can pull out the stops and have a really tough conversation:

1. You have to have authority in the person's life. Ideally, they would have given you permission already to have such a tough conversation. You are their leader in some fashion or a really close, trusted friend or have earned credibility over time in relationship, as Chris and I did with John.
2. Have the conversation in a way and in a moment when you think the individual might be able to hear it. Don't do it if you're angry or if the other person is in a bad place.
3. Have the conversation with only one intent in mind: love. Not to set them straight or show them what's up. It has to be with the heart of Jesus.

If you don't have these three things, don't have the conversation. If you do, go for it. Lots of prayer before, during, and after will help.

This week focus on speaking to others with both truth and grace. Be tough in telling the truth if need be, but season it with lots of grace. Don't use this chapter as an excuse to just go off on someone you're mad at. And if you're not sure what your motives are, ask your spouse or a very close friend before you dive in.

Jesus was full of grace and truth, but many of us tend to favor one or the other. Know your tendency. And be brave, in truth and grace, when the time is right.

CHAPTER FIFTEEN

Relinquish Control

Nonstarter: Overexplain yourself.
Opener: Let go and enjoy the ride.

EVEN JESUS TRUSTED GOD with the results of his ministry. He famously said, "I can do nothing but what I see the Father doing."[1] He was humble, fully confident, and totally secure. And he was completely dependent on God.

Here's one of my all-time favorite things about how Jesus operated: He would say something that confused or offended nearly everyone, and then he'd just keep going. No defense of his outrageous lines. No excuses. No overexplaining. Just a simple "Yep, that's what I said."

We see Jesus doing that constantly. Not worrying about the results. Not going out of his way to make people okay with him, not trying to convince people of the truth of what he was saying. Just being clear and faithful and leaving the results to his Father.

"Follow me," Jesus said to a young man. "But I have to bury my dad," the man said. "Let the dead bury the dead. You follow me," Jesus responded.[2]

"But I'm a professional fisherman," said Peter. "But I will teach you to be fishers of men," Jesus said.[3]

Jesus told people he healed not to tell anyone.[4]

He spoke to demons and sent them scrambling into a herd of pigs who jumped off a cliff and drowned.[5] Then he kept walking.

When Jesus' mom and siblings came for him, he asked, "Who is my mother, and who are my brothers?" and then pointed to his followers and said, "Here are my mother and my brothers."[6]

It would be a fun exercise to list all the outrageous, sometimes funny, and other times sarcastic things Jesus said without any explanation. We could surely find a hundred or more recorded in the Gospels.

Only a secure person could do what Jesus did. I know that when I'm insecure, I overexplain. I defend. I kick and fight and get mad and try to make others look dumb and myself look smart.

I can speak and leave the results to God only when I know that the whole world is in his hands, not mine. I'm not in control.

When we have total confidence in the sovereignty of a great and loving God who holds the universe together by his very breath, we can relax.

In every twenty-four-hour period, I take approximately eight hours off. Totally. No work. No thinking or planning or

strategizing. No meetings, no writing, no speaking, no helping, no serving. No anything. And guess what? Every single
day, I wake up and not only are his mercies new every morning but the world didn't implode. There is still air to breathe
and water to drink and ground to put my feet on when I roll
out of bed. God's got this. He created us and sustains us. He
holds everything together.

I'm constantly amazed at the reasons people give for not
having important conversations. They hold back for fear
they'll be misunderstood or because they think they don't
know enough to share about Jesus. This is pride in disguise.

If you do this, you're giving yourself too much credit for
convincing others about Jesus. You're not thinking enough of
God, not trusting he'll use you just as you are, with whatever
words come from your mouth.

The best way for us to get over pride and insecurity is to
allow ourselves to be moved by love and compassion, just as
Jesus was. To focus on the other person. To speak out of a
heart that genuinely cares. And then trust God to take care
of the rest.

I've spent much of the last twelve years telling my life
stories in written or spoken form. Not because they're so
great or because I'm so cool, but because they show how big
God is. Those who know me—I mean really know me—are
amazed that God could do what he's done through me. And
I'm amazed that God could do what he's done through me.
I'm serious. I'm a small-town country boy from Nebraska.
Graduated high school tenth in a class of twenty. I went to
a small college and got a simple BA in history. The most

important man I knew was my dad, and he was the pastor of a church in a small town. I never knew a mayor or a congressman or a rich person. I never could have imagined doing what I do now. I just wanted to hunt and fish and go camping on the weekends.

Yet I've discovered that God is big. And that he likes using people like me. And you. We're his surprise factor. We're the small hidden thing that his Kingdom emerges from. The little stone that becomes a pearl in his hand. The yeast that spreads to the whole lump of dough. Small and insignificant, until we're touched by God's Spirit. Then watch out.

What do we do? What's our part? We show up. We're full of courage not because we are strong on our own but because we're loved people. Loved by God, which in turn gives us the courage to love others. And that's the very thing that drives out fear, pride, and insecurity.

What does God do? Everything else. And you can drop the "else" part. Even the things we do are by his power. He literally gives us breath. So we open our hearts, minds, and mouths to love and serve those around us, in his name, with his power. That's it.

When you have a conversation, a good one, a tough one, one where you lay it all out, and then you drive home feeling stupid and insecure because you didn't do this or that right, let it go. It's God's deal. Don't be so intense. Chill a bit. Relax. God's got you and your conversations and the other person and their future.

Don't take yourself too seriously. Don't seek to be strong in yourself but rather trust strongly in God. Take a second look at the great "spiritual warfare" passage of Ephesians 6. You'd expect a lot of macho stuff. But not so. The section tells us that "our struggle is not against flesh and blood,"[7] and, in fact, it starts with the preface "Be strong in the Lord and in the strength of his might."[8]

What the passage does tell us to do, three times, is to stand. That's it. Stand. Get up. Wake up. Get out of bed. Whew, that's a relief. All that fighting and stuff could make a guy tired, but that's not our job. Ours is simply to stand.

But standing isn't always that easy. We get knocked off our feet every day by something in or around us. Life is hard. Getting back up and wading into the battle (the one God is fighting) isn't always a cakewalk. It's hard stuff, staying upright.

So don't take on any extra pressure. The weight of the world belongs with God, not you.

This week the challenge is to relax! And to stand. And trust.

Have the great conversations you're getting so good at and leave the results in God's capable hands.

The Final Word:
"Be Brave"

BE BRAVE. BE STRONG AND COURAGEOUS. "Yeah, but . . . " you say. "I would, but I'm not. The movie of my life wouldn't be *Braveheart*; it'd be called *Chickenheart*."

So to you, chicken-hearted friend, I want to ask you to do something: *stand*.

Do it, literally. Stand up right now, just for a second. You can keep reading, but just do it standing up for a bit. Feels good, doesn't it?

Standing firm and walking straight are such powerful metaphors. They're used repeatedly in the Bible to describe how the godly live their lives. We are told to stand and walk again and again. I'm assuming that's because God knows it's hard to stay standing, let alone walk with purpose. But just take some time to think about what it means to "stand firm."[1] To not give up. Don't worry about winning or conquering or doing something great. Just stand.

Winston Churchill once said, "Success is not final; failure is not fatal. It is the courage to continue that counts." You may have thought you were chicken hearted, but you're not. You wouldn't be reading this if you were. You have a courageous heart because you have been given the heart and mind of the bravest person who ever lived. You have the heart and mind of Jesus.

DIG DEEPER & DISCUSS

1. Who do you know who speaks boldly and courageously about Jesus in their interactions with others while also demonstrating kindness and presence? Describe a conversation you had with them or one that you observed.

2. Has anyone ever had an important conversation with you that probably required bravery on their part? What were the results of that conversation?

3. Read some of the Scripture passages referenced in this section (Matthew 16:21-25; Mark 1:29-38; 5:1-20; John 2:13-22; 8:1-22). What story or conversation of Jesus best demonstrates his courage?

4. This week we were challenged to be brave in our relationships with others. Which of the following did you attempt? How did it go?

   a. Think about what you are most passionate about in conversations and why. For what are you willing to speak up and bear the consequences?

   b. Think of at least one conversation in which you need to step out and be brave.

   c. Practice caring more about others than how you are perceived, even if you look foolish.

d. Practice speaking with both grace and truth. Know which one you tend to favor.

e. Relax and leave the results to God.

5. Are there one or two people in your life with whom you should have wise, careful, but brave conversations soon? Decide who those people are and prayerfully develop a plan to move forward. Get counsel from a trusted friend if you're not sure how to proceed. (And remember, bravery is not an excuse to be harsh and unloving; it's a call to simply do what needs to be done in the most Christlike way possible.)

4 Be Jesus

We must never allow the authority of books, institutions, or leaders to replace the authority of knowing Jesus Christ personally and directly. When the religious views of others interpose between us and the primary experience of Jesus as the Christ, we become unconvicted and unpersuasive travel agents handing out brochures to places we have never visited. BRENNAN MANNING

May they also be in us so that the world may believe that you have sent me. I have given them the glory that you gave me, that they may be one as we are one—I in them and you in me—so that they may be brought to complete unity. Then the world will know that you sent me and have loved them even as you have loved me. JESUS, JOHN 17:21-24

I don't know exactly why you decided to read this book, but I assume that if you've come this far, you are serious about making some sort of difference in the lives of the people with whom you come in contact. You care enough about Jesus, and others being introduced to him in small and large ways, to put a fresh magnifying glass to his life and, in particular, his conversations. And that is what we focused on in the first three sections: following Jesus in his kind, present, and courageous conversational ways. Seeing the title of this section, you may have wondered, *Isn't "being Jesus" what you've been challenging us to do all along the way?* Well, yes. But in this final section, I'd like to go even deeper.

Jesus gave us the ultimate example in everything. But that is not all he gave us. He promised his first followers, and those who would come after them (a.k.a. *us*), that he would give them himself, actually be *in* them. The actual presence of Jesus is in us, which means that we can be the actual presence of Jesus to others. Not because of our own good works or perfection, but because of his gracious and generous gift of his presence and love to us.

Paul actually says that we are being transformed into Jesus' likeness. But this transformation is not a passive process on our parts. It requires intention, reflection, and pursuit. Not, as we talked about in the previous three sections, toward others in our conversations, but toward Jesus himself. To become like him so much that we believe, act, and love like he did: consistently, from the inside out.

The challenges in this section will take on a different feel. They will not be so much related to what you do in relationships with others but rather to what you do in relationship to Jesus, the Father, and the Spirit. As his ways become your ways, his very life will flow out of you to others.

CHAPTER SIXTEEN

Do I Believe What Jesus Believed?

Nonstarter: Assume Jesus believed like you do.
Opener: Discover what Jesus believed and adjust accordingly.

JESUS BELIEVED STUFF. About himself. About his Father. About the world, sin, life, heaven, hell, people, religions, and politics. He had what we'd call a belief system.

I grew up with a Western Christian worldview, which reflected the beliefs of American evangelicalism and our interpretation of Paul's beliefs more than what Jesus actually believed. So it wasn't until later in my life that I even thought to ask, *For a follower of Jesus, wouldn't it be most important to understand what he believed, especially if we want our actions and interactions to mirror his?*

For the first half of my life, I made the assumption that the beliefs espoused by the church of my upbringing matched those of Jesus. Not necessarily.

I want to list here what I think were some of Jesus' beliefs. The following are taken directly from my friend and long-time mentor Bart Tarman. There are twelve beliefs in his list, but Scripture shows us many others as well.

1. Jesus believed that God is like a daddy.
2. Jesus believed that faith is the key to opening every door—not correct thinking but childlike trust.
3. Jesus believed in love.
4. Jesus believed in humility.
5. Jesus believed that dying is the key to living.
6. Jesus believed that everyone is welcome.
7. Jesus believed that the best life is lived in community.
8. Jesus believed in being generous.
9. Jesus believed that change comes from the inside out.
10. Jesus believed in an upside-down Kingdom. An opposite world. If you're rich, you're poor. Be friends to enemies. Live to die. Be a child to be mature. Become empty to be full. Forgive to be forgiven.
11. Jesus believed in empathy—treating others the way we want to be treated.
12. Jesus believed in forgiveness, received and given.[1]

Do any of these beliefs surprise you? Do you disagree with any? If not, let me ask, do you believe like Jesus? I would call these beliefs principles of God's Kingdom, similar to the law of gravity. They're true and can always be counted on,

100 percent of the time. But only if we believe and act upon them will we see any impact on our lives and the lives of those around us.

You might be familiar with the ongoing discussion among philosophers, sociologists, and theologians about the order of progression respective to behavior, thoughts, and beliefs. If you had to draw a flow chart of those three things, what would it look like? I would argue that our beliefs come first. That our beliefs lead to our thoughts (beliefs are the underpinnings of our thinking). And that our beliefs and thoughts are expressed in our behavior. Unfortunately, Christian discipleship often focuses on modifying behavior (don't sin, do pray, and so on) more than dealing with our thoughts. And my experience has been that our discipleship seldom gets all the way down to our core beliefs.

Let's take a deeper look at the first core belief of Jesus. In the previous section, we saw how Jesus was able to say or do hard things and then trust his Father with the outcome. This faith rested on his deep knowing of the Father as a loving Abba (daddy). So much so that in his time of greatest struggle in the garden of Gethsemane, the night before his crucifixion, he was able to call out to God as Abba. This core belief grounded him in his darkest hour. Does it do the same for us?

We may profess to believe that God is a loving Father, but if in our hearts we perceive him as distant or scornful (or negative in some other way), we'll find it very hard to trust him in the risky, painful, and dark times of our lives. And that will manifest in our interactions and conversations, despite our best attempts, conscious or unconscious, to mask it.

It's what we believe in our hearts, not what we say with our mouths, that makes up our core beliefs.

And our core beliefs lead to our thoughts, which lead to our actions. You can tell what others really believe by watching how they live. People who perceive God as truly loving, trustworthy, welcoming, generous, forgiving, and empathetic act consistently with those beliefs. They can readily admit when they've screwed up because they know that God loves them and can be trusted to help them. They can laugh at themselves. They don't take themselves too seriously because they know God's "got them." They hold possessions loosely and give generously because they experience him being generous with them.

If you want to follow Jesus in all your actions and interactions, can you see how important it is to believe as Jesus did?

We've all lived out of wrong beliefs. I grew up feeling like a loser. I wasn't cool. Not smart. Not athletic. Not especially talented. My impression of God, though I wasn't conscious of it at the time, was that he was harsh and demanding. And that affected my whole life. All my decisions. I spent all my time and energy trying to prove to myself and others that I was worth something. I became a really hard worker and took on the toughest of tasks, which earned me kudos from others, but I also became driven and crazy busy. This mentality hurt my family, almost ruined my marriage, and damaged many of my friendships. This pain and dysfunction all stemmed from the false belief that I was unworthy and that God was a hard taskmaster.

Thankfully, I'm being reoriented to believe what Jesus believes. We call that healing.

And it is good. Very good.

What if you and I agreed that this week we would begin immersing ourselves in the beliefs of Jesus with the intention of believing those same things? Start by reviewing the twelve beliefs of Jesus and asking him to help you believe those things as well. As our minds and hearts are transformed to be like his, our actions will follow. I expect the life of Jesus—in love, generosity, welcome, empathy, and so much more goodness—to influence those we interact with in powerful ways.

CHAPTER SEVENTEEN

Do My Words Match My Actions?

Nonstarter: Talk big.
Opener: Act bigger.

JESUS DID A LOT OF TALKING. And as we've seen in some previous chapters, he said some pretty outrageous things. But he walked his talk. He lived with integrity.

When the disciples were afraid of the stormy sea, Jesus rebuked them for their lack of faith. Which was shocking in itself. Big talk. But even bigger, he then proved they had no reason for fear by calming the storm and demonstrating his power over the sea.

Jesus famously said, "Greater love has no one than this: to lay down one's life for one's friends."[1] Beautiful words. Strong words. Poetic and unrealizable words, we might think, except for this one fact: He did it. He called us friends and laid down his life, in the most painful and public of ways, for us.

His words and actions always lined up.

Jesus warned his followers, "The teachers of the law and the Pharisees sit in Moses' seat. So you must be careful to do everything they tell you. But do not do what they do, for they do not practice what they preach."[2] Don't you love that? He honored the Pharisees' position and their teaching of God's law, and he instructed his disciples to obey that law. But Jesus also instructed the disciples not to imitate the actions of the Pharisees because they were hypocrites.

I deeply desire, and try, to live a life of integrity, but my words don't always match my actions. I might speak at a conference about the importance of being a humble servant like Jesus, then return home and "forget" to take out the trash. Or I commit to following up with a friend on some big issue in his life but unintentionally forget, getting so busy with my own life to make the call. Or I say I'll pray, but I don't.

I'm human. I fail. But I do my best to ask forgiveness and keep trying when I realize I've screwed up.

You see, we earn authority with others—the ability to speak into their lives—when our actions match our words. When we demonstrate trustworthiness and integrity with preparation, thoughtfulness, and follow-through.

I recently went for coffee with a young man I'd gotten to know over the previous few months. He poured out his heart to me—about his dysfunctional family, substance abuse, difficult marriage, and lack of life direction.

Chris and I had been spending time with him and his extended family, just listening and praying with them. We'd stayed in their home and had welcomed them into ours.

After the young man talked for a good hour about how bad things were—most of which we already knew—he asked me, "So what do you think I should do?" I had been praying specifically that he'd ask that exact question and that God would give me a helpful answer. He did ask, and I was ready.

"You need to stop seeing those friends. Say goodbye to them. Literally. Now. You need to ask your wife to forgive you for these three things you did. Do not take another drop of alcohol, and stop the pot, today. And here's who can help you do that. And commit to knowing Jesus. Read the Gospels five times. Spend fifteen minutes a day reading them. Pray each day with your wife, even if it's for ten seconds. Listen to these twenty online messages and take notes. That's it for now."

He was in a bit of shock. I'm not sure what he thought I was going to say, but I went for it. I finished with this: "Sam, you know I love you. I love your family, and we are your friends for as long as you'll have us. I want to help you. How about if you write me a little e-mail once a week just telling me how you're doing with these things? I won't be tough on you. Do them only if you want to. It's entirely up to you. And I will engage with you as much as you engage with me. I'll call you, e-mail you, visit with you, whatever you want, as long as you do these things. If you choose not to do them, that's fine, but I won't help you. You'll be on your own. Clear?"

Guess what? He's done all I've asked and more. It's been almost a year, and his life has changed. I was able to challenge him as I did because he'd heard me preach and heard me talk and then he watched how Chris and I live and saw that my words matched my actions. I told him many times that I cared. But, much more impactful, I demonstrated it by being ready to speak with authority, wisdom, and clarity when the opportunity came.

Of course, I can tell you many similar stories that didn't turn out that way, either because I didn't have the kind of authority I thought I had, or the person just refused to listen, or I just wasn't prepared.

This week let's do some self-reflection, asking ourselves how often our actions match our words. Do you tend to talk bigger than you walk? Maybe consider asking some trusted friends and family members for feedback. Do you have the authority that comes from living a life of integrity? Or are there areas of hypocrisy that need to be revealed and confessed?

We all know the adage "Actions speak louder than words." Let's be ready for those expected and unexpected interactions by building a track record of integrity that goes before us.

CHAPTER EIGHTEEN

Do I Really Know Jesus?

Nonstarter: Speak only of facts and doctrine.
Opener: Speak from personal encounters.

WAIT, CARL, YOU MIGHT BE THINKING. *We're trying to help* other *people know Jesus. Of course I know Jesus!* Good point. You wouldn't be reading this if you didn't know Jesus in some capacity or weren't at least curious about him, so much so that you actually want to talk with other people in a way that is Jesus-like.

Nevertheless, I want to press a bit into this idea of *knowing* Jesus. Especially in light of the emphasis of this section, which is knowing and encountering him in such a way that we are transformed into his likeness. Able to be Jesus to someone else.

Jesus knew his Father, and he demonstrated for us a life of intimate, unbroken connection with him. Look at just some of the examples we have of Jesus pulling away to be alone with his Father: before he chose the disciples; when he grieved the loss of his friend and cousin, John the Baptist; and, of course, the night before his crucifixion. Where did Jesus go when he needed wisdom, comfort, or courage? To be with his Dad. His knowing went so deep, he even said that the words he spoke were not his own but belonged to his Father. Wow.

Now, you may be thinking, *Yeah, but Jesus had it easy. He is God, after all. You know, the whole Trinity thing. Of course he knows his Father. They're one.*

Well, I have a "Yeah, but" to throw right back at you. He was fully man, too. He modeled for us the best way to live. And he actually invites us to the same kind of deep, connected knowing of himself that he had with his father.

So back to our question: Do we really know Jesus?

We toss the word *knowing* around fairly easily. There's a big difference between knowing stuff *about* Jesus (we call that doctrine, and it's good—very good—but it should never stop there) and knowing Jesus.

After reading this book, you'll know a lot about me. And you could read my other books and listen to all my messages online and know quite a few things about what makes me tick. You'd know some of my hopes and dreams and what I think of God and life. You'd know that I'm married with three kids and that we live much of the year in the Middle East. Yet if someone asked you the simple question "Do you know Carl Medearis?" you'd have to hesitate. You'd say something like "Well, I mean, I 'know' him. Sort of." And you'd have to explain that we've never actually met. And if we had met at a conference somewhere, you'd still have to explain that you actually don't know me well.

I know my closest friends. I have their phone numbers and they have mine. We text. Call. E-mail. Meet up. I've been to their homes and know their families, and they know mine. When they're not doing well, I know it. And when I'm having a struggle of some kind, they're there for me. We're good friends. Not everyone can be like that. For me, it's really just a few handfuls that would be considered such close and intimate friends, such that I'd say I "know" them.

This is the kind of "knowing" we need to nurture with Jesus. True friendship takes time. It takes some bumps along the road. Some ups and downs and that unique feeling of missing someone when you haven't seen them in a while. It takes physically spending time with them. It is a little harder with Jesus since he's not physically with us in the way you and I could be with each other. But he's with us in every other sense of the word *with*, and in many ways it's a deeper *with* than we can experience with those who are physically present.

As I pointed out in the introduction to this section, not only did Jesus use *with* to describe his connection to us, he used the word *in*. We can remain in him, as he will remain in us. Like branches connected to a vine. Growing fruit is impossible without that connection. Separating the branches from the vine leads to withering and death. That's the knowing I'm talking about, which Jesus modeled for us as he related to his Father. Deep, intimate, life-source connection.

I experience Jesus in a multitude of ways. In prayer. Silence. On a walk in the woods by myself. I experience him profoundly in the midst of community. During worship and singing. I think I experience Jesus most deeply in service, especially to the poor. When I read the Scriptures, he often leaps off the page. In fact, I take seriously his proposition that "if you remain in me and my words remain in you, ask whatever you wish, and it will be done for you."[1] Something about his words, the actual red ones we see in some Bibles, knowing them inside and out, seems to be an important way to really know him.

When I open myself to God in all these ways, I get to know him more and more.

But this is not always easy for me. Relationships, even with God, can be difficult. And time consuming. And sometimes I hear things that I don't really want to hear. Sometimes it feels easier to go it alone. Keep him at a distance. Do my own deal. In case it isn't clear by now, I can be selfish with my time and affection. However, there is a perfect participant in this relationship who hasn't given up on me yet.

Giving ourselves to knowing Jesus more and more will transform our hearts, our service, and, of course, our conversations. And we have a lifetime (and more!) to get to know him. Remember, just after Jesus' crucifixion, when he walked incognito on the road to Emmaus with two disciples? He spoke to them from Scripture of all the places Jesus was mentioned. And once they realized who he was, they expressed how their hearts had burned within them as he spoke.

I can't help but think that when we know Jesus, truly

know him, and when we've given ourselves to knowing his words so that they are in us, there will be a power to the words we speak to others that goes way beyond literary impact.

This week take some time to get away with Jesus. Spend time, perhaps more time than you are used to, to be with him. Go for a walk with him. Read his words and meditate on them. Maybe even memorize them. Speak them to someone else. Ask him to help you know him more. Jesus himself said that we will find him if we seek him with all our hearts. There could be no better payoff for our effort, so let's do it!

CHAPTER NINETEEN

Do I Do
What Jesus Did?

Nonstarter: Shrink back from suffering.
Opener: Pray for the sick and afflicted.

JESUS WENT AROUND HEALING THE SICK, casting out demons, raising the dead, and preaching the Good News of his new Kingdom. And he told his followers to do the same.

If we're at all serious about being like Jesus in our interactions with others, we must take seriously what he instructed us to do. Disciples not only have conversations like Jesus did but also act like he did, which means we reach out to bring healing.

Jesus never said, "Pray for the sick"; he told his disciples to "heal the sick."[1] I know, I know—that sounds intensely Pentecostal, as if I'm some crazy preacher with slicked-back hair on late-night cable TV. But I'm just telling you what Jesus said. And any attempts to make miracles sound like they were just for Jesus and his original twelve apostles don't hold water. The books that come after the Gospels show followers of Jesus fully embracing this call, this vision of the new Kingdom that included healing the sick, casting out demons, and raising the dead.

I'm not a big faith-healer guy. Sick people don't always get well when I pray . . . and I don't pretend that they do! I don't see any need to raise my voice or draw out the word *God* into something with three syllables: Ga-wa-da. He knows what I'm praying, why I'm praying it, and what to do about it. I don't try to manipulate him to heal by the cleverness of my words or how they're pronounced.

But just because those faith healers on TV seem to be full of hype and manipulation (in my humble opinion), I can't discount the instructions of Jesus to heal. And here's why:

- God is able to do whatever he wants whenever he wants. So if he wants to do a miracle of any kind, he's free to.
- God is mostly doing miraculous stuff wherever I'm not—such as Africa and South America— places where people are generally more open to the supernatural, as opposed to the Western part of the world, where people tend to be highly rational and dismissive of the supernatural realm.
- God, every once in a while, does do something wildly miraculous when I pray. God loves to come and touch people through prayer. If people aren't healed, they

almost always experience being touched by his love, which is also a kind of healing.

Wouldn't Jesus still be moved by love and compassion today that brings wholeness to the lives of suffering people, just as he was when he walked the earth?

I believe in healing because I've experienced it. I've seen people set free from lifelong addictions and from the effects of very hurtful experiences. I've seen very sick people healed and the lame walk. I've experienced God's power come as I've been moved by his love and compassion.

Now, to be clear, God doesn't always make himself actively known when I pray. And I don't know why people sometimes get healed and other times they don't. There's a lot that we can't know about why suffering occurs; it's a complex combination of the enemy's activity, our choices, and things going on (in the heavenly dimension) that we can't see. We don't know how much God can override the laws he's set in place without compromising the stability they provide—how much he can intervene without overriding our free will and responsibility. And Scripture teaches us that there are other factors that influence the outcome of our prayers, such as what God's will is in the situation, how many people are praying, the faith we are praying with, and the presence of sin. But just because we don't understand how God works through prayer doesn't mean it's not a vital action as we connect to those around us.

You're probably wondering, *Okay, Medearis, what does performing miracles have to do with having a nice chat with my neighbor?* Glad you asked.

Let's say the nice over-the-fence chat with your neighbor goes like this:

"Hey, Carl, what's up?" your neighbor asks.

"Not much. You?" is your wise, pithy reply.

"Well, actually I just got back from the doctor and I have a tumor."

So there you go. What do you do with that one? All of a sudden your friendly chat has turned into something pretty serious. Your neighbor begins to tear up and you feel helpless. I am not suggesting you hop the fence, place your hand on the tumor, and say, "Be gone in Jesus' name." But I'm also not encouraging silence. Oh, and believe me, I've gone that route many times. Someone is sick or just got some horribly bad news and I let out a feeble, "Oh, I'm so sorry to hear that." I'm chicken, I guess. Or I don't really believe. Or I just had a fight with my wife and I feel depleted of anything that would smack of Jesus' authority. Or all of the above.

Is there a good alternative to either saying nothing or giving your best and most awkward televangelist impersonation? Again, so glad you asked. Yes, as a matter of fact, there is. And that way is surprisingly like Jesus' way: naturally supernatural.

We're not confronted with the need for physical healing every day, or even every week. But I'd venture that most people in our lives regularly need some level of healing, whether the wound is visible or not. Your neighbor, friend, coworker, or family member might share something with you—a health scare, emotional pain, relational brokenness—that requires a miracle to correct. First of all, be human about it and simply listen. Hear their hurt and pain. Cry with them if they're crying. Give a hug if it's appropriate, and sit down to listen some more. Don't offer counsel or make medical prescriptions. Just be a good friend.

And then, ever so naturally and normally, ask if it's okay if you pray for them right then. Very few will turn down prayer in such circumstances. Why would they? Even if they're not sure about God or his abilities to do miracles, they figure, *Why not try?* What do they have to lose?

Sit down with them somewhere comfortable and make sure they feel okay with you praying. Then you might ask if they mind you placing your hand on their shoulder or back or knee or wherever they're hurting, if it's a physical concern. In my humble opinion, this is not so much of a theological necessity as it is an act of faith on your part. It shows that you actually believe in what you're about to do. And it shows kindness toward the person. The touch of a warm, friendly hand is a bit of healing in and of itself.

Be brief. Don't make it awkward for the person. Preserve their dignity. This is so important. I've seen so many would-be healing pray-ers work themselves into a "faith frenzy" at the expense of the person they're praying for. Don't try to convince God (or yourself) by raising your voice or being verbose. Don't tell them they are healed in Jesus' name.

Just simply ask Jesus to come and heal. Invite him to do what only he can do and what he loves to do. He brings life. Healing and wholeness.

And just like with the rest of our conversations, we leave the results up to him. Praying for someone who's sick or hurting or afflicted by the demonic (having nightmares, being plagued by terrible thoughts, feeling afflicted, being tormented in some way) isn't about us. It's not about us looking good or doing or saying exactly the right thing. It's simply about loving the other person. Praying for the miraculous in a real-life situation with another person is the supreme act of faith, hope, and love. It is a part of having conversations like Jesus did.

This week go find someone to lay your hands on. Gotcha! Just kidding. Don't force it. Instead, talk with God about how you feel about healing and miracles. What you are afraid or unsure of. Perhaps do a little math and count all the times Jesus healed someone and how many times his followers in the New Testament were part of blessing others with healing and miracles. Then ask God to prepare you to be ready for the next interaction, the next opportunity, he gives you to be part of bringing healing and life to someone else.

CHAPTER TWENTY

Do I Live as if Jesus Matters More Than Anything?

Nonstarter: Set your spiritual cruise control.
Opener: Make the difficult choices.

SO HERE WE ARE, coming to the end of the book, but hopefully engaging with a whole new way of thinking about how to talk with people. If you've been practicing the challenges while reading, you are well on your way to learning by experience.

But we are not done yet. In fact, I've left the toughest question for last: Do you live like Jesus matters more than anything?

Jesus knew he mattered. He claimed to be God. He claimed to be "the way and the truth and the life"[1]—the only way to God and to eternal life. He asked people to be his disciples and said things like "You cannot be my disciples if you do not do what I say."[2]

He famously instructed his disciples just before his death to go and encourage all the world to believe in him, follow him, and obey his teachings. Jesus was clear about his identity and mission and the importance of his life.

But here's the thing: Jesus responded to his importance and purpose very differently than many of us would.

Rather than swell with pride or lean toward self-dependence, Jesus stands as our example of truest humility. Jesus' realization of the importance of his life and ministry propelled him toward necessary and intentional intimacy with his Father in heaven. That intimacy resulted in full obedience to the will of his Father. Jesus' dependence went so deep that he said he spoke and did nothing on his own, but only what his Father told him.

I imagine that this was not always easy for Jesus. He had to make some extraordinarily tough decisions because his life mattered so much. And each of those decisions was lived out in dependence on the Father.

I think of the night Jesus was arrested and Peter chopped off the arresting officer's ear. Jesus rebuked him for using the sword and then said, "Do you think I cannot call on my Father, and he will at once put at my disposal more than twelve legions of angels? But how then would the Scriptures be fulfilled that say it must happen in this way?"[3]

Jesus knew he had the option to avoid the painful trial of crucifixion and death before him. Shortly before the ear incident, he had talked with his Father, pleading with him to "take this cup"[4] away. He knew the choice he needed to make. In the deepest of trust and submissive obedience to the will of his Father, he said, "Not my will, but yours be done."⁵

We all long for significance, to know that our lives matter in the big picture and to God. Jesus experienced that. His life mattered more than anyone's. But Jesus knew that the key to fulfillment of his highest purpose and calling was not willpower, intelligence, or a long-term strategy but rather intimate connection with his Father and trusting submission to his will. And if Jesus needed it, who are we to think that we don't?

I don't always relish this idea of dependence. I like being my own boss. The captain of my own ship. I accepted a role with an organization a few years ago and for the first time in about twenty years, I had a boss I had to report to. Rough. I still struggle at times. I can't help but wonder if Jesus—because he was a man, tempted in every way like we are—sometimes struggled with the whole dependence and obedience thing. Not sure. But if we believe that Jesus matters, if we believe that following him matters, we will follow him right into the humility of dependence and obedience.

Several years back, when we were living in Lebanon, I believed God was calling me to an act of radical obedience. It was a crazy idea (because, as we know, Jesus sometimes leads us to do and say crazy things). It was going to require trust and utter dependence on the Father. And there was really no good reason to do it—unless I really believed that Jesus matters, and that trusting obedience was the smartest, wisest move.

I felt compelled to give a personalized New Testament

to every member of parliament (MP)—all 128 of them. Very few people thought this was a good idea (and they let me know). My own thoughts argued against it. It didn't make sense according to the mission strategy we had chosen at the time. It was too high profile and could lead to our getting kicked out of the country. So many reasons not to do it.

But I couldn't deny that God had spoken to me in an unusually clear way. Louder than the voices telling me I shouldn't. Deeper than my own logical thoughts that argued against it. The "still small voice"[6] deep inside assured me, as much as I knew, that this was the will of my Father, and my role was to obey and trust.

It was hard. Hard to make the Bibles with personal inscriptions. Hard to raise the money for it. Hard to make the appointments. All very, very hard. But I pressed on and formed a small team who helped me. I would make the appointment, go meet the MP in their office, and explain what I was doing. I'd give them the Bible and then ask if I could pray for them. Almost all said, "Yes, please."

I had about fifty of these appointments . . . and then we got kicked out of the country. Still, undoubtedly, the most traumatic event of our lives. And not a few friends said, "I told you so."

Was it worth it? I really don't know. I've admitted that my Bible-passing-out thing is probably what led to us being booted, but would I have changed that if I had known? I don't think so. In fact, I hope not. I don't even know the positive (or negative) outcomes of those fifty

New Testaments I handed out. I've seen only two of those MPs since. But God knows.

This whole book is about learning how to have conversations like Jesus had, and living as if he really matters, more than anything else, will transform so much more than our conversations. If we believe that Jesus matters, if we really know him as King of a new and real Kingdom to which we belong, if we trust and depend on him as King of our lives, we won't be able to just read this book and walk away. We'll spend time really getting to know him through Scripture; we'll learn the rhythms of his life; we'll cultivate a longing to be more like him. To know his voice. To discern his will. And when we do, to yield to him in trusting obedience.

One of my heroes, for obvious reasons, is Mother Teresa. A friend of mine got to meet her at one of the homes she ran in Calcutta a few years before she died. She was just coming out of her morning prayer time (which began at 4:00 a.m., by the way), when she sat down on a little bench to chat with my friend and his companions (who all happened to be very important college students).

"Mother," my friend asked, "how do you do it? How do you keep on serving in the face of so much suffering?"

Without blinking, she looked at him and answered with confidence and sincerity, "I love Jesus like a new bride loves her husband."

That's it: ten simple words. (She had this 42 seconds thing down!) Her love for Jesus propelled her to live a life of radical obedience and devotion to the poor. For her, Jesus mattered more than everything else.

My friend, this big, macho college-football-player type, has been chewing on her words for the past twenty-five years. This interaction changed him.

This week ask yourself and Jesus, "Is there any place in my life where I am walking in disobedience? Is there any situation in which I am not living out of dependence? Do I really believe that Jesus matters?" Ask for strength and help to follow him with trusting abandonment in whatever he asks. Choose to live like Jesus matters, more than anything, and your decisions, conversations, and life will never be the same.

The Final Word:
"Be Jesus"

WELL, WE'VE TRAVERSED lots of territory together, learning to talk and interact and engage as Jesus did. And as I promised (and hope you experienced), the challenges became progressively more difficult and personal.

That was intentional. You see, "being Jesus" to others is actually our goal. And it's not always easy. Being Jesus implies a losing of ourselves. And who likes to lose?

Jesus gave us fair warning. This following Jesus thing, if we're really going to do it, requires a death of sorts. "Whoever loses his life for my sake," said Jesus, "will find it."[1] True life. In Jesus. With Jesus. That's what I want, and I'd imagine that's what you want if you've made it this far and are still tracking with me.

And because Jesus loves the world (yep, everyone in the world—not being dramatic here), he wants true life, for us and for all we come in contact with. As his friends (that's what he called us), we get to be part of his great and beautiful purpose of drawing all people to himself—by showing him to the world, by being Jesus to the world. Yes, it costs us something, but, I think we agree, the reward is great.

So, you see, the first three sections were appetizers to the main course, so to speak. (Really good ones, I might add.)

We've discovered how simple kindness—just saying hi, looking people in the eye, asking questions, starting with small acts of kindness, paying attention to people's kids—can open the door for deeper conversation.

We've discussed the gift of presence: moving from self-absorption, past our own insecurities, to give the gift of ourselves. We've learned to see what's really going on with others, see beneath the surface, and risk relaxing and asking questions in order to deepen our conversations.

We've looked at places where bravery is required—how we need to choose our "barley fields," where God has given us conviction to take a firm stand, and how we can determine when it's a good thing to stand alone in those convictions. Hopefully, we've taken risks to speak truth as well as grace and learned to trust God with the results when things don't go as we desire or expect.

And in this main course, we've considered what it looks like to be intentional about being transformed into Jesus' likeness so that we can be his powerful and loving presence in this world that needs him. We've been challenged to take an honest look at how we relate to Jesus. Do we believe what he believed and live with integrity? Do we spend the time to really know him, not just *about* him? Do we really believe that his power to heal resides in us? (He did say we would do greater works than he did.) And finally, do we live each day acting and interacting with the awareness that Jesus—and his will—matters more than absolutely anything?

I don't know about you, but the thought of "being Jesus," of representing him and showing him to others, humbles me like nothing else. I'm thankful he knows we're on a journey, that we are made of "dust"[2] and make mistakes. And I'm glad he sees in you and me more than we see in ourselves. Just like he saw in Peter. But, as he did with Peter, he invites us to take the risk, step out on the waves, and come to him. And to be transformed so that we might be his healing presence in this world.

Are you ready?

DIG DEEPER & DISCUSS

1. Take another look at the beliefs of Jesus listed in chapter 16. Do you struggle with any of these? Which one(s) and why? What have you believed instead?

2. When was the last time you got away to be with Jesus, to know him better? If recently, what is something he is speaking, or has spoken, to you? If it's been a while, when can you get some focused time away?

3. This week we were challenged to dig deep into our life with Jesus and see ourselves and our interactions change as a result. Which of the following did you attempt? How did it go?

   a. Immerse yourself in the beliefs of Jesus. Where is there alignment? Where are there contradictions between his beliefs and yours?

b. Do some self-reflection and ask yourself, and maybe some trusted friends, "Are there areas of hypocrisy in my life? Places where my words are bigger than my actions?"

c. Spend some time really looking at Jesus' words. Meditate on them. Maybe even memorize them.

d. Ask God to prepare you for the next opportunity you will have to be a vessel of healing in someone's life.

e. Evaluate if there are any places of disobedience to Jesus in your life. If so, confess and move forward in obedience.

Epilogue:
The Final, Final Word

JUST 42 SECONDS. The average time of Jesus' conversational interactions in Scripture. I consider it pretty thoughtful of Jesus, really, to keep it so short. He must have known, being omnipotent and all, that we twenty-first-century Western people would be so busy with all our important work that anything more than 42 seconds may cause even more anxiety in our crazy world.

Thank you for taking this journey with me. It means a lot that you would trust me to guide you toward being more like Jesus and making a difference in the lives of people you interact with every day. As I've thought through how best to communicate this information to you, it's refreshed and challenged me as well.

Before we walk away, I'd like to give three very practical examples of the types of ordinary 42-second interactions that most of us encounter on a daily basis. They are probably not my most memorable examples, but they are real and recent, so I thought I'd share. I pray that each one is a shot of encouragement to use the ordinary moments of your life the way Jesus did.

ARMAN AT THE LIQUOR STORE

You know those people you see throughout your day? I'm not talking about family and friends or even acquaintances, necessarily. I'm talking about the ones you run into briefly every day: the cashier at the grocery store, your kid's soccer coach, the people who wait on you at the dry cleaner's, the receptionist at your work. These are the people who make up the tapestry of your day, the faces you might recognize but don't know well. And you can so easily change the tone of your interactions with them just by practicing the Jesus way.

A few months ago, I needed to pick up a bottle of wine. We were having some friends over for dinner and wanted something nice to go with our summer barbeque. So I went to the liquor store closest to my home, looked around, found something that would work, and brought it to the checkout counter. As I got ready to pay and head home, I started to chat with the man behind the counter. He obviously hadn't been in America for very long, so I asked him his name, where he was from, and other basic things. It turns out that his name was Arman, he and his family were from Iran, and they were Muslim. The conversation continued something like this:

> ME: "Arman, I thought Muslims weren't supposed to have anything to do with alcohol. And you run a liquor store?" (I said this with a smile on my face and a knowing twinkle in my eyes.)

ARMAN: "Well, my family is Muslim because we're from Iran. That's just how it is. This is good business. I'm not very religious."

ME: "Oh, okay. That makes sense. I'm not very religious either."

ARMAN: "Aren't you a Christian?"

ME: "Well, yes. That's my background. Just like you're from a Muslim background. But I'm really not very religious. I just try to follow Jesus."

ARMAN: "I thought you said you weren't very religious."

ME: "Right. And neither was Jesus, really. He never got along with the religious authorities. Isn't it funny that we think of him as one now?"

ARMAN: "Huh. Well, have a good evening. Enjoy the wine."

And that was the end of it. All in all, it lasted about four minutes. Since then, I've been back to that liquor store about six times. Four of those times, Arman was at the counter. We're starting to build a friendship. Every time I'm there, I bring up something about Jesus.

For some of you, it's not normal to strike up a conversation with somebody and immediately get to religion, personal devotion, and following Jesus. However, it *is* normal to frequent a local store or business. We all have people like Arman in our lives who we see occasionally. Maybe not every day, but we'll probably bump into them again. I try to make it a point to frequent the same places so I will run into them again . . . and again. And over time, as you share bits and pieces of your life and learn about theirs, it will be natural to speak the name of the one who means most in your life. Just start there.

McDONALD'S ON A ROAD TRIP

A substantial chunk of your daily interactions are with people you have almost no chance of ever seeing again. Let's say you're driving across the country to visit family for the holidays. Exhausted, you and your family fall out of the minivan and stumble into McDonald's with hopes of some caffeine and a working restroom. There's no line because it's nearly midnight. You walk up and talk to the cashier.

This moment seems like nothing. The person in front of you doesn't seem to matter nearly as much as how fast they can serve you a ninety-nine-cent coffee. But in reality, this person bears the image of God as much as any piece of creation ever made, and you have no idea what your moment with them can mean. Think of Jesus and the woman at the well in John 4. It too was a quick, random interaction, but Jesus seized the moment and changed an entire village.

You won't transform a town at 11:39 p.m. in a McDonald's along the interstate, but God probably has more in mind for that moment than you do.

Most of these people are used to folks walking and driving past them all day long without ever looking up or saying hello. You can easily add a loving touch with a simple, "How are you?" or "Did you know that God really loves you?" You might not change your McDonald's cashier's life, but you have a great deal of power to add to their day.

What about that person sitting next to you on the airplane? Or the occasional repair man who comes out to your house?

Even if you did have some idea of what your minute of attention would mean to the person in front of you, you'll never know what God is up to in their life. What if God is ganging up on them with his love and you're next in line? They might encounter five hundred people over the next ten years who all follow Jesus and act as though they do in their little interactions. That has the power to change a life.

TEXTS AND TWEETS

We've spent most of this book talking about our ordinary interactions with people in person. But we need to remember that a lot of our ordinary interactions take place on social media. And even though there is a string of devices between us, a living, breathing person is sitting on the other side of the screen.

If you take all of Jesus' interactions, translate them into English, and count up the number of characters, the vast majority fit into a text or tweet. In fact, the "opener" in each section of this book is less than 140 characters. You could dismiss what you put on social media as entirely unimportant or without impact, but I doubt that Jesus would feel the same way.

Yes, you can still put up a status about how nice the weather is or a picture of your cat getting stuck in the bathtub. But don't minimize the potential for the virtual realm of the ordinary to make a difference in somebody's day—or life. Whether your voice in the virtual world of your "friends" is small or large, are you taking advantage of that window to nudge the people listening in the right direction? If somebody read everything you put up, would they learn more about what it means for Jesus to be a part of your life? Would they be better able to follow Jesus by following your posts?

One incredibly practical way to go about these interactions is to add depth to the sensational. We love things that stir our emotions, make us perk up either in enthusiasm or in disgust when they come across the screen. The latest controversy, the most amazing new technology, the biggest celebrity faux pas. People constantly brought things to Jesus' attention that riled them up one way or another. They would ask him how they ought to act under an unjust government, bring up national tragedies and wait for his commentary, and highlight the most amazing architecture in Jerusalem. Consistently, Jesus seemed to hear what they said, take a step back, and give his input on the deeper issue. And we can follow his example.

So whether you're the most extroverted person in the world or painfully introverted, every day you have moments, interactions, with *people* who cross your path. And you have a unique opportunity, a calling, to be like Jesus in those moments and to those people. It doesn't have to be awkward. It doesn't have to be weird. And it doesn't have to be long. You just have to take the first simple step. A step toward another person. A step in following this Jesus you love.

In fact, it might take only 42 seconds.

NOTES

BE KIND

1. Galatians 5:22, esv

CHAPTER ONE:
SAY HEY

1. See Matthew 4:18-22; Mark 1:16-20;
   Luke 5:1-11.
2. See John 4:1-26.
3. See Matthew 19:14.
4. See Luke 24:13-35.

CHAPTER TWO:
ACKNOWLEDGE THE WAITER

1. See Matthew 9:18-26; Mark 5:21-43;
   Luke 8:40-56.
2. See Matthew 9:18, esv.
3. See Mark 5:22, esv.
4. Luke 8:49, nlt
5. Mark 5:36; Luke 8:50

CHAPTER THREE:
ASK ANOTHER QUESTION

1. John 5:6
2. Mark 10:51
3. John 21:17
4. Matthew 12:48
5. John 8:10, nlt
6. Matthew 16:15
7. See 2 Corinthians 5:17;
   Revelation 21:5.
8. John 3:7

CHAPTER FOUR:
DO SOMETHING SMALL

1. See Isaiah 53, nasb.
2. See Luke 21:1-4; Matthew 15:22-28;
   Luke 18:35-43.

CHAPTER FIVE:
TALK TO THE KID

1. Matthew 19:13-15; Mark 10:13-16;
   Luke 18:15-17
2. Matthew 18:5, esv

CHAPTER SIX:
BREATHE DEEP

1. See Genesis 16.
2. See Genesis 16:10-12.
3. See Genesis 16:8.
4. Genesis 16:13
5. Genesis 16:13

CHAPTER SEVEN:
STOP TRYING TO BE COOL

1. Luke 4:22, esv
2. See Luke 4:25.
3. See Luke 4:26.
4. See Luke 4:27.
5. *Merriam-Webster Online*, s.v.
   "vulnerability," https://www
   .merriam-webster.com/dictionary
   /vulnerability.
6. Brené Brown, "The Power of
   Vulnerability," YouTube video,
   20:49, posted by "TED," January 3,
   2011, https://www.youtube.com
   /watch?v=iCvmsMzlF7o.

CHAPTER EIGHT:
OPEN YOUR EYES AND EARS

1. Matthew 16:1
2. Matthew 16:2-3
3. See Mark 10:17-31.
4. Mark 10:17
5. See John 4:35.

CHAPTER NINE:
ACCEPT THAT YOU ARE NOT GOD

1. *Merriam-Webster Online*, s.v.
   "humility," https://www.merriam
   -webster.com/dictionary/humility.

CHAPTER TEN:
DON'T BE SO STRATEGIC

1. John 6:53
2. John 6:60
3. John 6:61

4. John 6:66
5. See Luke 5:17; 8:26; 23:49.

THE FINAL WORD: "BE PRESENT"

1. Matthew 6:11, ESV

CHAPTER ELEVEN:
FIND YOUR BARLEY FIELD

1. 1 Chronicles 11:12-14
2. See John 8:2-11.
3. See Matthew 12:1-14; Mark 2:23-28.
4. See Luke 10:38-42.
5. Matthew 16:23, ESV

CHAPTER TWELVE:
STAND ALONE
(WHEN NECESSARY)

1. See Matthew 8:14-15; Mark 1:30-31; Luke 4:38-39.
2. See Matthew 8:16; Mark 5:1-20.
3. Mark 1:33
4. See Mark 1:36-37.

CHAPTER THIRTEEN:
SAY SOMETHING CRAZY

1. See John 9:6.
2. See John 2:19-20.
3. Exodus 9:1
4. Ruth 1:16
5. See Hosea 1:2-3.

CHAPTER FOURTEEN:
BE FULL OF GRACE (AND TRUTH)

1. See John 2:4; 7:6; 7:30.
2. See John 8:7.
3. See John 8:9-11.
4. See John 8:19-21.
5. See John 8:39-40.
6. See John 8:41.
7. John 8:43-44
8. John 8:48
9. John 8:58, NLT
10. See Matthew 22:36-40.

CHAPTER FIFTEEN:
RELINQUISH CONTROL

1. See John 5:19.
2. See Luke 9:59-60.

3. See Matthew 4:19.
4. See Mark 1:43-44; 7:36.
5. See Matthew 8:28-34.
6. Matthew 12:48-49
7. Ephesians 6:12
8. Ephesians 6:10, ESV

THE FINAL WORD: "BE BRAVE"

1. Ephesians 6:14

CHAPTER SIXTEEN:
DO I BELIEVE WHAT JESUS
BELIEVED?

1. Bart did a twelve-part sermon series on these beliefs that would be well worth your time to listen to: http://summerlandchurch.org/sunday-mornings/12-beliefs-of-jesus.

CHAPTER SEVENTEEN:
DO MY WORDS MATCH
MY ACTIONS?

1. John 15:13
2. Matthew 23:2-3

CHAPTER EIGHTEEN:
DO I REALLY KNOW JESUS?

1. John 15:7

CHAPTER NINETEEN:
DO I DO WHAT JESUS DID?

1. See Matthew 10:7-8; Luke 9:1-2, 6; 10:9.

CHAPTER TWENTY:
DO I LIVE AS IF JESUS MATTERS
MORE THAN ANYTHING?

1. John 14:6
2. See Matthew 16:24; Luke 14:26, 33.
3. Matthew 26:53-54
4. Mark 14:36; Luke 22:42
5. Luke 22:42
6. 1 Kings 19:12, KJV

THE FINAL WORD: "BE JESUS"

1. Matthew 16:25, ESV
2. Psalm 103:14